REVEALING THE UNSEEN HAND

GOD'S PROVIDENCE DOCUMENTED

To Orvil and Betty

LEE R. CLENDENNING, PHD

Lee R. Clendenning

Dedicated to my grandchildren

Victoria Leigh Clendenning
Sterling Leigh Clendenning

Copyright © 2013 Lee R. Clendenning, PhD.
www.revealingtheunseenhand.com

All rights reserved. No part of this book may be used or reproduced by any means, graphic, electronic, or mechanical, including photocopying, recording, taping or by any information storage retrieval system without the written permission of the publisher except in the case of brief quotations embodied in critical articles and reviews.

WestBow Press books may be ordered through booksellers or by contacting:

WestBow Press
A Division of Thomas Nelson
1663 Liberty Drive
Bloomington, IN 47403
www.westbowpress.com
1-(866) 928-1240

Because of the dynamic nature of the Internet, any web addresses or links contained in this book may have changed since publication and may no longer be valid. The views expressed in this work are solely those of the author and do not necessarily reflect the views of the publisher, and the publisher hereby disclaims any responsibility for them.

Scripture taken from the King James Version of the Bible.

Any people depicted in stock imagery provided by Thinkstock are models, and such images are being used for illustrative purposes only.

Certain stock imagery © Thinkstock.

ISBN: 978-1-4908-0698-3 (sc)

Library of Congress Control Number: 2013915945

Printed in the United States of America.

WestBow Press rev. date: 9/9/2013

Contents

Foreword v
Preface vi
Acknowledgments viii

Chapter 1: Beginnings 1
Chapter 2: Primary and Elementary Learning 16
Chapter 3: My Family Changes Churches 26
Chapter 4: Living and Learning—Middle Grades and
            Junior High 30
Chapter 5: Summer, 1954—Salvation Realized! 42
Chapter 6: Going Steady for Years—Early Ministry 45
Chapter 7: Beginning High School 48
Chapter 8: 1956-1957, Junior Year—Life Changing Accident ... 56
Chapter 9: God Provides a Scholarship 66
Chapter 10: Sharing Married and College Life Together 71
Chapter 11: 1963-64, Master's Degree Program in Ohio 89
Chapter 12: 1964-1965, Public School Teaching and Parental Care 93
Chapter 13: Life in New Jersey—Montclair State College 99
Chapter 14: Life and Teaching in Wisconsin—Stout State
            University 106
Chapter 15: PhD. Studies—University of Illinois, Urbana ... 116
Chapter 16: Living and Teaching in Virginia 133
Chapter 17: The Move to Georgia—Berry College 141
Chapter 18: Administering the Industrial Education
            Department 151
Chapter 19: Taking Care of the Family 160
Chapter 20: People to People Goodwill Ambassador for
            Vocational Education—Europe and Russia 163

Chapter 21: Building a Long Term Home 184
Chapter 22: Promotion and Tenure.. 186
Chapter 23: Fun with Family "All work and no play
 makes Jack a dull boy." 190
Chapter 24: Leading a Vocational Education Delegation
 on a Chinese Scientific Exchange 195
Chapter 25: Completing a Career 221
Chapter 26: Finding a Church Home in Georgia 223
Chapter 27: Health and Family 225
Chapter 28: The Unseen Hand Has Been Revealed!..................... 229

Foreword

Dr. & Mrs. Lee Clendenning invite you to journey with them through a lifetime of blessings from God. *"Revealing The Unseen Hand—God's Providence Documented"* is a testimony of how God has His hand on the lives of these precious people. Whether they were working on a farm or teaching on the college level, God always directed their steps.

I have had the privilege to serve as the Clendenning's Pastor since 1999. They are not just "born again," they are "practicing Christians." Their reputation in the community is outstanding. When you hear the names "Lee" and "Patricia" you think of high moral standards and integrity.

Lee and Patricia love children. Parents anticipated their children entering 3rd grade. That's because the Clendenning's would be their Sunday School teachers. The crafts in Vacation Bible School were the best because the Clendenning's designed them.

They have a compassionate heart for people. When a member of our church faced surgery, our staff would hear from patients: "Lee and Patricia came early today to pray with us." Often times this visit was made before Lee reported to teach his 8:00 a.m. class at Berry College.

I recommend this special story Dr. Clendenning has written. He opens the doors of their lives and traces God's providence for you to enjoy. What a refreshing testimony in a day of self-helps and secularism, the Clendennings have the courage to say "God is the source of our strength and blessings." You will be encouraged by reading this book. What God has done for this couple He stands ready to do for you.

Philip May, D. Min.
June 18, 2013

PREFACE

The "Lighthouse" and the "Unseen Hand" are metaphors referred to by Christians to explain God's guidance and provisions for our lives. Christians sing about the Lighthouse figuratively illuminating the path to salvation. The action of His Unseen Hand controls events in the background so that ". . . all things work together for good to them that love God, . . ." (Romans 8:28). Verify this truth repeatedly as you are following the inspiring events of a life-long Christian which take a poor, barefooted seven-year-old from harvesting in bean fields with migrant workers to walking the Great Wall of China as the leader of a delegation of Americans representing vocational education. Watch God fulfilling the prophesy of Isaiah 35:8; to open up a way so plain that ". . . wayfaring men, though fools, shall not err therein."

Revealing the Unseen Hand—God's Providence Documented is also a love story, describing how two thirteen-year-olds with complementary skills started together in friendship and shared ministry which continued through courtship, over fifty years of marriage, and a challenging, but fulfilling academic career. Providential revelations and solutions to immediate and long term problems appeared in wondrous, if not miraculous ways. I am compelled to share with others, especially my grandchildren, the knowledge of these events, documenting God's love and care. Strengthen your faith as you reflect on your own lives and find meaningful fulfillment. Smile and widen your understanding of what common life was really like for many of us who grew up in rural America in the middle of the Twentieth Century. Gain insight into the American academic community and enjoy first hand observations of life behind the Communist Iron and Bamboo Curtains at the height of the old "Cold War."

In the narrative the actual names of some people who were very important to me, or that I wanted to especially honor are identified. However, in general, throughout the work, providing specific names of many people was not necessary for understanding the truths of the story. In most cases, people are identified by their title or descriptive role.

Only enough information about my immediate forebears to expose the roots of my character and faith is presented. Those interested in a detailed family tree should study elsewhere. This narrative is not an extended diary. The early chapters describe events generally in chronological order. However, some of the later chapters summarize overlapping experiences covering a period of years. The narrative is not exhaustive. Some experiences are too personal to share publically, and many would be of no interest.

Acknowledgments

I am deeply indebted to my wife, Patricia, for her faith in me, support as a helpmate, friendship as a soul mate, encouragement to tell the narrative, and for her memory and personal notes which greatly improved the accuracy of reporting. I am also indebted to Diane H. Campbell for providing editorial services including proof reading and advice on questions of grammar, inclusion of content, and structure of presentation.

Chapter 1

Beginnings

"Before I formed thee in the belly I knew thee; and before thou camest forth out of the womb I sanctified thee . . ." (Jeremiah 1:5a)

On October 6, 1940, Mother travailed with me as the small town doctor and his assistant made their way to our home. The doctor was surprised at the call because he had assumed that I had already arrived without his assistance. On the only prenatal visit in late August, he had told my expecting parents that Mother could safely deliver at any time. According to Dad's account, the doctor explained that the new procedure of induced labor allowed much greater freedom in the timing of deliveries. Since the doctor was planning a late summer trip into New York's Adirondack Mountains, he gave them some pills to take home with them. He specifically warned them not to take the pills until the next day. Dad was a practical, hard-headed New England farmer who believed that birth was a natural process. Mother and Dad had experienced the five previously successful home births of my sisters, Dawn, Ruth, Rita, Sylvia, and my brother, Andy. Dad threw the pills into the wood-burning cook stove. Years later, Dad would chuckle wondering how long the doctor anticipated his call.

Over six weeks later, the doctor finally got that call. Fifteen miles on the old unpaved roads took a while back then, but the Lord got him to us in time to untangle the umbilical cord from around my neck. He saved me from immediate death or a life of brain damage due to the lack of oxygen. Home births had such hazards. Mother was openly proud that she had not lost any of her children.

When I was a creeping baby, my life was saved again. Early in my parent's marriage, Dad started construction of a small home in the bottom of the valley on the farm homestead. By the time I was born, it was an unfinished shell accommodating a kitchen, living room-dining room combination, the promise of a future bathroom-laundry facility, and quite open family sleeping areas in an attic space. As a part-time blaster, Dad kept black gun powder and dynamite on the property. Somehow, gunpowder had gotten spilled onto the floor of the house without being noticed. As was her common practice, Mother dumped the floor sweepings into the fire in the stove. The explosion set fire to Mother's clothes and nearby interior wall surfaces. My oldest sister, Dawn, was home that day. She immediately ran to get Dad who luckily was working with the old tractor in the closest field across the creek. While my siblings scattered outside, I was trapped in a small crib. A neighbor with a team of horses happened to be passing by when the explosion occurred. The neighbor entered the flaming house and carried the crib, with me in it, out across the creek. Dad's old tractor was prone to overheating, so Dad always carried a water pail with it. He scooped up water as he came across the creek. The neighbor helped Dad put out the fire with another water pail.

Mother was temporarily blinded and burned badly around her face, right breast, upper arm and shoulder. There was no 911 service in those days. Dad rushed Mother to Memorial Hospital in Cortland, New York, approximately twenty-five miles away, as fast as a vintage 1920's vehicle could go. For a number of weeks, I was cared for by my Aunt Marion (Perry) Haskins, Mother's sister, in De Ruyter, New York, while Mother fought the inevitable infection. Though only ten years old, Dawn supervised the rest of the children at home. Many times, Mother mentioned how pleased she was that I recognized her and started creeping right for her when she was finally able to come for me.

As I reflect on the orally reported recollections from my parents and siblings about my birth and the gunpowder blast, I have always marveled at how close I came to not being here. Those events, many less life-threatening experiences, and my survival of a botched heart by-pass operation in later years, have convinced me that God does have a plan and purpose for my life. I am still attempting to follow that plan as best as I can discern it.

The hill territory where I was raised

The ancestral farm homestead of my family consisted of over 350 acres in the middle of New York State, and had been handed down within the family for generations. We enjoyed five fresh water creeks and springs and drank freely from any of them. The main stream was the headwaters of the Tioughnioga River. The farmhouse afforded a building site with a view up, down, and across the valley. Except for one flat meadow of five acres, most of the land was steep hillsides, pasture, and woodlands. The ridge north of the home featured a very long sled, ski, or toboggan ride if one had the energy to climb it in the winter snow.

After the death of my grandparents in the early 1940s, the homestead was divided among my father and his two sisters, Doris (Clendenning) Foster and Elsena (Clendenning) Haines. I do remember the surveyors working to divide the property, even though I was too young to have had any idea what they were doing or why at the time.

Farming in this area as I remember it as a child in the 1940's was only a small step away from pioneer living. The farm provided milk, eggs, meat, and vegetables in abundance, even for a big family. However, these provisions came by the sweat of the brow. Children were free labor, so families of eight to a dozen children or more were not uncommon. There were six children in our family during this time. Everyone worked at chores appropriate to their age and abilities. My first chore was to gather the eggs. Since chickens were allowed free-range to scrounge for weed seeds and bugs in the garden, every day was like an Easter egg hunt. Human labor and horses still provided much of the prime power, but Dad managed to get an iron-wheeled Fordson tractor. The neighbors had different pieces of farm machinery which they freely shared at work bees; so everyone's crops got planted, silos got filled, grain harvested, and winter wood cut. Women held quilting bees and took their knitting to social events like Farm Bureau meetings. We made our own candles from beef tallow and our own soap from lye and lard. Cold running water existed in most kitchens, but out-houses were still commonly used, even serving the churches. Cold springs, ice boxes, and root cellars provided refrigeration. We were at the very end of lines delivering electrical and telephone service. In emergencies, we accommodated folk living further back in the hills. Cash flow was tight. Generally one member of the family took at least a part-time job beyond the farm.

Paternal Grandparents, Andrew Clendenning and Rena (Allen) Clendenning

My grandfather, Andrew Clendenning, was born on the homestead, the son of a Canadian immigrant and Eva Mary (Parker) Clendenning. She was one of the daughters of Dwight and Hannah Parker who owned the farm at that time. The following spring after Grandpa's birth. Eva Parker died apparently of anemia. Grandpa's father returned to Canada, leaving his son on the farm to be raised by his Parker grandparents. The Parkers worshiped in the Quaker Basin Church, two miles down the valley west of the homestead. By Dad's report, as an adult, Grandpa did not formally worship. He was known to be a very honest, hard worker.

Andrew Clendenning married my paternal grandmother, Rena (Allen) Clendenning, a "town" girl who, by oral accounts, apparently never really accepted or enjoyed life on the independant and somewhat isolated farm. Her father, J. D. Allen, ran a plumbing and tinning store in De Ruyter, the closest town. Grandmother Clendenning was determined in the pursuit of personal goals. She physically did the carpentry to add a sun porch as an eastern entry to the home. The porch included windows downstairs and an open veranda upstairs. She built a carport to shelter her 1924 Chevrolet coupe from sun and rain. As I was being trained in traditional principles of wood framing and finish carpentry, I found her work quite crude and unorthodox; but the projects served their functions for years after her death. Maybe she carried the genes which affected my love of physical structures.

Maternal Grandparents, John Perry and Encie (Aldrich) Perry

My maternal grandfather, John Nelson Perry, was an itinerant holiness preacher. Some members of his large clan were lumberjacks who moved from region to region harvesting the abundant virgin forests in Central New York and Northwestern Pennsylvania. When he was a boy, some of the Perry clan lived on the flat top of the ridge, northeast of the Parker homestead.

Family lore says that Grandfather John Perry's first marriage lasted only one night. After this, the bride returned to her family, and the marriage was annulled. At some point, he married my grandmother, Encie Aldrich, who is described as a quiet, long-suffering saint. It was reported that she was an excellent seamtress and had a green thumb with flowers and plants when she was in one place long enough to tend them. Other than her raising six children, including my mother who was the youngest, and following dutifully wherever her husband went, often in a covered wagon, I know little about her.

After John Perry was saved and called to preach, he traveled with his growing family by horse and wagon as far west as Terre Haute, Indiana, north to Port Huron, Michigan, where Mother was born, south to Huntsville, Alabama, and finally back to the Central New York area. Mother's older sister, Aunt Marion (Perry) Haskins, described the children amusing themselves in the back of the wagon. They made faces at local children knowing that they would never see them again.

By all accounts, Reverend John N. Perry was a loud and powerful preacher. Typical of many holiness preachers in his day, he had no formal theological training and distained preparing formal sermons. God's spirit was trusted to fill his mouth with the right message for the occasion. The tale of his unfortunate first marriage eventually followed him wherever he went. In the holiness culture, this mistake apparently precluded his acting as a long time pastor.

Reports of Reverend John Perry's personal life were not very positive. He had strict expectations of all around him, including his children and animals. It was said that he worked the horses to their physical limits. Sensing when a team was about ready to stop in rebellious exhaustion, he would holler "WHOA" because he did not want them to stop without permission. His only son, my Uncle Julian, said that his father never treated the whole family at the ice cream parlor at one time. Instead, he would take each of the six children for a treat individually, thereby enjoying much more ice cream than any one of them. He was troubled because his five daughters married men, including my father at the time, who did not profess to being born again Christians. He was quoted as saying, "The devil owed me a grudge and paid me off in sons-in-law." Mother said that while she and Dad were courting, she deliberately expressed interest in another suitor who used tobacco in order to make Dad look better by comparison.

Mother, Mildred (Perry) Clendenning

Whatever her father's faults may have been, Mother did accept the positive Christian principles that he preached and that were exemplified in the lives of the good common folk in the small country churches where he served. She passed these values to her husband, eventually seeing my father confess Christ as his savior, and to my generation. I owe my faith and whatever God has accomplished through me to the foundation that Grandpa Perry started and Mother passed on to me.

Mother completed eight grades in school which was all that was expected of girls in her culture who were not aspiring to be teachers. She was an excellent oral reader and entertained the whole family by the hour reading the Bible and novels to us on cold winter nights. She was a hard worker who always prepared excellent meals each day for the family. In addition, there was always laundry (without automatic washer, dryer, and permanent press clothes), cream to churn, chickens to dress, gardening, seasonal canning, and sewing. During World War II, Mother worked at the B. F. Gladding fish line factory in South

Otselic, NY, which was converted to make parachute cord. After the war, she worked as a cook in the local schools.

Mother had a passive personality. Like me, she was the youngest in the family and conditioned not to pick a fight which she was sure to lose. In addition, the folks preaching the holiness doctrine of "entire sanctification" felt that most shows of anger were a sign that the devil was still in charge of one's spirit, or an indication of undesirable rebellion. In that culture, an angry childhood tantrum was not tolerated. Her people practiced the Biblical admonition, "Withhold not correction from the child: for if thou beatest him with the rod, he shall not die. Thou shalt beat him with the rod, and shalt deliver his soul from hell." (Proverbs 23:13 & 14) Dad liked to quote those verses even before he had made a personal religious commitment. I soon learned that even if I were foolish enough to get angry, I sure was not foolish enough to let it show if I could help it. There were very few times when Mother let her "righteous indignation" show. Mother normally left the physical aspects of discipline up to Dad. (I now know that the inability to show honest anger and thus "clear the air" can have its own long-term negative effects in relations with others.)

Mother was not very affectionate with us. I do not remember hugs and kisses, but, I never doubted that she loved me. She was thoughtful. We put ourselves to bed and got up and dressed ourselves. Yet, on a suddenly cold night, she might appear with an extra blanket and tuck us in. If the bath water was cold by the time my brother, Andy, and I were in it, (we were always last) she would have hot water from the tea kettle on the stove to warm it for us. She always prepared our favorite desserts for birthdays and on other special occasions.

As we each started school, Mother expected us to behave and never to cause trouble. We were expected to pass so that people would know that we were not "dumb" (her term). If we achieved anything beyond passing, we had to be self-motivated. I never recall her asking if homework was completed, or even if we had any assigned.

Mother was a quiet perfectionist. She expected all tasks to be performed correctly without the need for false praise or even honest cheerleading after achievements. She would quietly point out that the Christmas tree we had cut was not symmetrical, or the branches were scrawny. If I painted something, she could find the brush streak. Few people really recognized her inner perfectionism because she kept it well hidden beneath a very socially pleasant persona. She never nagged or badgered and very seldom complained.

Father, Allen DeLee Clendenning

My dad, Allen D. Clendenning, was a sharp contrast to Mother. He was assertive about his likes and dislikes regarding everything from hog feeding to national politics. Both Dad and his sister Elsena had polio as children. The disease left Elsena partially crippled. Dad's case was milder, leaving him with a slight limp only noticeable when he tried to run. At the age of thirteen, he was blinded in one eye by a flying nail as he was repairing a fence. Dad completed the tenth grade in school before concluding that he was "as smart as his teachers." From that point, he considered schooling a waste of time except for women who needed it to become employed in the school system. Apparently sometime in his youth, he developed a case of hypochondria. He had one continuous ailment or another from common colds to diarrhea and aches and pains in his bones and joints for the rest of his days, sometimes missing months of work. He had his own medical theories regarding various conditions and his own special treatments which he often imposed on the rest of us. In one of my earliest memories, I asked Mother why she was putting pills in Dad's lunch. She replied that they were for his "tooth-ache in his heel." I later learned that he believed he had arthritis in his foot bones spread there from tooth decay by the circulation of his blood. Following this theory he had all of his and Mother's teeth pulled, and they used false plates before I was born.

Dad's courtship of Mother started from a chance meeting with her brother after not seeing him for years. When Mother and was a young girl, the Perry family rented a small home near the Clendenning homestead before moving on to another community. The family was apparently out of Dad's consciousness until his early twenties when he had a chance meeting with her brother, Julian Perry. As the two young men reminisced, Julian asked Dad about his date life. I understand Dad replied that he didn't believe any girl would go out with him. Julian arranged a double date with Dad, his sister Mildred, and Julian's current girlfriend. Courtship and marriage followed soon afterwards.

Dad took pride in being a "jack of all trades." He completed a Chicago-based correspondence course in electricity which equipped him to install and repair wiring in local farms and homes. He had a natural mechanical aptitude and trained himself in auto mechanics and the repair of farm machinery. He worked much of his time in those fields. For years, he drove school bus and worked a second job between runs.

Dad expected his children to act and work as small-scale adults. A significant portion of my grade school and early teen time outside of school was spent working on tasks he had assigned, or working with him on one job or another. This work, from dynamiting stumps to cabling together structurally failing barns, gave me a very unusual practical education. I had "hands on" practical skills needed to operate the farm and to work in the carpentry, mechanical, and electrical trades. At home, Andy and I worked most often without him at everything from daily dairy chores to building fences, planting, cultivating and harvesting, butchering, and cutting needed winter wood. Often Dad's teaching method was to assign work and leave us to figure out how to get it done. This did greatly enhance our problem solving skills and gave us confidence in our own abilities. Occasionally he was upset by our solutions. Cutting down a tree for fence posts was a prime example:

Dad: "Boys, tomorrow, cut down some black cherry trees to make fence posts."

We: "How big trees should we cut?"

Dad: "It doesn't really matter. We will have to split them anyway. The bigger the tree, the more posts can be split from it."

Result: The next day we searched the acres of forest to find the biggest black cherry tree there. Then it took all the rest of the day to cut it down by hand with ax and cross cut saw. Dad came home from work late in the afternoon. Not finding us home yet, he came the half mile into the woods to check on us. The tree came crashing down just as he arrived. It was 39 inches across the stump and 24 feet up to the first limb. According to his ranting and raving, we had cut "The most valuable tree in the woods!" It was only then that we learned what he had in mind was a tree ten to 12 inches in diameter which could be easily split two ways making four posts for every six feet of length.

In spite of his lack of interest in religion in the early years of his marriage, Dad had social ideas which were compatible with Mother's holiness background. Any type of "Demon rum" was to be avoided totally. If one never took the first taste of alcohol, one would never be an alcoholic. Carbonated soft drinks were considered just a first step toward stronger beverages. If one never took the first puff or chew, tobacco addiction was avoided. He disapproved of the physical contact between the sexes associated with any kind of dancing. Therefore, he sent notes to school forbidding his daughters from participation, even in folk dancing. My sisters could not go to the Junior Prom, the Senior Ball, or any of the round and square dancing events sponsored by local fund-raising groups. Cosmetic make-up was a waste of money.

Like many males of his generation and culture, Dad harbored very definite ideas about the roles and expectations of the sexes. The farm naturally divided work into women's household chores and men's barn and field work. Music was fine for girls. They could take piano lessons. Real men didn't sing, even in church. Husbands were to support their wives. In inconsistency, Dad assigned some of his daughters to outside chores when they were home and often assigned me to "rustle up some grub" for lunch. He could be heard singing as he worked if he thought nobody else was around.

Siblings Dawn, Ruth, Rita, Sylvia, Andy, and Daniel Clendenning

Being the youngest member of the family for thirteen years, I only know what I was told about the early life of my siblings. Sometime following my birth, my oldest sister, Dawn, moved away from home for the first time to work for her room and board. Her responsibility was to care for an elderly lady in town. Dawn was nine years old. After the woman's death, Dawn was home and gone intermittently until moving to Cortland to work her way through college. Ruth did much less outside farm labor. As a creeping baby, Ruth crawled under the running washing machine and mangled her fingers on one hand in the belt drive pulley. This precluded her milking cows. In high school, she alternated working weeks with Dawn at Mable Crump's nursing home in town. She always seemed to have homework to do when it was chore time. She was the only one who could use that dodge. Upon high school graduation, she did win a lot of academically related honors, and went on to become a degreed nurse. Rita was the most rugged of the sisters, and worked the most outside with Andy and me. In high school, she took over the nursing home assistance as Dawn and Ruth moved on. After high school, Rita became a registered nurse. Sylvia did housekeeping and nanny work for families in the community.

The sisters considered me a "Go fer"; "Go upstairs and get my hair brush from the dresser" (or anything else they thought they needed at the moment). They called me "Baby Lee" until I was six years old. I would complain every time. They set my place at the table with a tin plate and cup until I got old enough to bury those utensils out in one of the fields. I helped my sisters look for my plate and cup with a straight face. Nobody ever figured out what happened to them.

Andy was my "big brother" even though I cannot remember when I was not actually physically taller and heavier, but never stronger, than him. I understand as a toddler he had some sort of digestive problem that forced him to regress to baby food which may have stunted his growth. Andy was my playmate, best friend, and co-worker. We always shared a bedroom, and in our younger years, the same bed. I learned a lot from watching his successes and mistakes. Andy and I did have friendly wrestling matches in the naturally padded hay mow. We also had downright serious fights which I never won. He was naturally quicker in temperament. All was always forgiven and forgotten by the time we had to enter the house. Andy was also my spiritual leader. When he quietly started daily Bible reading, I decided it was time to do the same.

Early memories

We must have been considered really poor or unfortunate by outsiders. The Christmas following the gunpowder explosion which burned Mother, the De Ruyter American Legion Post delivered toys and other gifts to our family. Andy described my fear of a toy army tank when it spit sparks moving in my direction. That is why I have always had an appreciative spot in my heart for the American Legion. Although I did not sense the poverty at the time, many of my early hard lessons were related to our economic condition.

Another indication of the poverty was the conservation of soap. All laundry loads were run through the same wash water in a sequence from the white bed sheets, then my four older sisters' clothes, then Dad's work clothes with any play clothes Andy and I had soiled. With laundry finished, Mother would take out the machine agitator without draining the water and lift Andy and me into the tub for our bath. The water by then was usually pretty dark, or blue if the overalls were reasonably new. I wondered why the girls were not bathed this way. Mother said they were too big to fit into the tub. We had a splashing good time! Seriously, I got one spanking for leaving a purchased cake of soap to dissolve in the hand wash basin. I came to understand that "bought soap" was expensive. In the same way, I learned not to leave light switches on if I was the last person to exit a room.

Mother shopped regularly for clothes and household items she might find at the Salvation Army Thrift Store. She was a good seamstress and often made and mended our clothes. Hand-me-downs were the rule, and often we were given used clothing from cousins. As I grew older, she taught me the elements of clothing repair. I was never a tailor, but the skills she taught me were very useful as I was completing the required textiles course in college.

All of us kids, by personal choice, went barefooted most of the time when the weather permitted. One did have to watch out for dead thistle prickers and "Cow Pies" in the pastures. At the time, we had no inkling that we should feel sorry for ourselves. My sisters told about a county social worker showing up, apparently checking on the proper care of the family. When she expressed sympathy for their lack of shoes, they were proud to show her their "Sunday" shoes. Her surprise apparently amused them.

On Sundays, Mother loaded all of us children into the 1924 Chevy coupe inherited from Grandmother Clendenning, and we went to

Sunday school and church. I had a wonderful pre-school teacher, Mrs. Irene Hinds, who taught us songs and gave us pictures. I still remember "Praise Him; Praise Him; All you little children. God is love; God is Love." And of course, "Jesus Loves Me." One sunny day on the way home from church, Mother called back, "Do you want to see what it is like to go 30 miles per hour?" Of course we did! We thought we were flying! Dad never went to church with us. He said he could sleep more comfortably at home.

During family excursions with Mother, I usually ended up sitting on somebody's lap in the rumble seat because there were no child seats or seat belts back then. In the cold of winter, Mother provided wrapping blankets for us. Dad kept tire chains on the car during the worst of the winter. They provided the "rumble." If a tire cross chain came loose on one end, it would fly up and hit the underside of the fender with every turn of the wheel; CLANK, CLANK, CLANK until we got home. Apparently, no one anticipated the personal danger we were in if the loose chain happened to penetrate into our riding area.

For a time, between the death of the Clendenning grandparents and the final division of the property, the homestead house was rented to a family larger than ours. I remember spending time playing with their children. When the tenants moved out, we moved into the big homestead, and our Little House became part of the property allocated to Aunt Elsena and Uncle Louis Haines. Aunt Doris and Uncle Lloyd Foster inherited the farm on top of the hill to the east.

The tenants had left a serious problem. Bed bugs! They bit us every night, and we were tormented with itching. Dad tried stripping us down and spraying us with rubbing alcohol before going to bed. No help. He tried disinfecting the rooms, the beds, and the bedding, and nothing worked. Finally, in desperation, he had Mother get metal bed frames and headboards from the Salvation Army. These he scorched thoroughly with a blow torch to kill possible eggs. Then he burned the old wooden beds in a bonfire. Dad laid the old mattresses out on the lawn, poured kerosene all the way around the exterior of each one, and quickly set fire all around. I can still see his pleasure as he watched the bed bugs appear from hiding and run to the middle of the mattresses in an attempt to escape. With new bedding, we were finally bed bug free!

Lee R. Clendenning, PhD

Ending my brief, carefree childhood

The first couple of years after moving into the big house continued my carefree childhood. Much of the time, Andy and I, completely unsupervised, roamed the fields, creeks, and woods. We climbed trees, caught frogs and salamanders, and looked for snakes; there were no poisonous ones in the area. We picked wild berries and ate them on the spot. We cooled off in a deeper place in the main creek. The highest structural beams above the haymow in the big barn became our perches before jumping to a soft landing below. We used carpenter tools to bore holes in barn beams just because they were there and tried driving nails just to see if we could. We used hatchets to chop on trees in the pasture just for the fun of it. In the winter, we slid downhill and enjoyed snowball fights.

There is an old saying, "The devil finds work for idle hands." This was finally true for Andy and me, and our "deviltry" on one summer day put an end to childhood as I had enjoyed it. We took some matches from the kitchen and tried to build a fire in a makeshift stone stove in a field out of sight of the house. Failing at this, we entered our old home (Little House in the valley) through a cellar hatchway. The cellar had a dirt floor and some stored kindling wood. We just got a fire going when the hatch suddenly opened. A whirlwind in the form of a BIG man appeared. Without saying a word, he kicked our fire apart, stomped it out, and left us in bewildered shock. It was my Uncle Lloyd Foster, husband of Aunt Doris, who noticed smoke while he was splitting firewood across the road. He told his wife who promptly informed Mother about the fire. By the time we were slinking home, Mother was looking for us. I will never forget the mixture of righteous indignation and disappointment on her face when we arrived. Using a weapon about the size of a thick yardstick, she quite properly beat our backsides into total repentance and resolution to be better behaved in the future.

When he got home, Dad sentenced us to greatly increased chores to occupy our time. To harness our interest in fire, we were made responsible for keeping the fires in the cook stove year around and in the house furnace in cold weather from 6:00 a.m. until bedtime. This included bringing ten or twelve armloads of wood from the woodshed every day and cleaning out the ashes every week. Barn chores were also increased.

Andy and I become piano tuners

At some point before Andy and I started school, Mother took a job on the second shift in the B. F. Gladding Fish Line Factory (converted to produce parachute cord) in South Otselic, ten miles away. The problem was that she had to leave at 2:00 p.m. and the school bus did not bring our sisters home until 4:00. Andy and I were totally unsupervised for two hours each weekday afternoon. We were expected to wash, rinse, dry, and put away whatever dirty dishes there were in the kitchen (working from step stools). We could play the remainder of the time. One day Dad hired a man to tune the piano. We were intrigued by his taking apart the piano to reveal the "duck heads" bobbing back and forth as the keys were struck. We watched him strike a key while listening intently, make some correction with a special wrench and then repeat the process. It looked like fun. After doing the dishes that afternoon, we decided to play piano tuner. There was no sinister motive. We mimicked the tuner's actions. But, it was a BIG upright piano, big enough for us to open the top and climb in on top of the duck heads. We really did not notice that our feet had broken a couple of them. After tiring of this activity, we went on to some other way to kill time.

When the school bus came, Dawn rushed in, sat down and soon discovered the non-working keys. We were convicted of deliberate mayhem without a trial. Knowing what was coming, I hid behind the couch waiting for Dad to come home when he finished the bus run. Andy faced his fate "like a man." When Dad finished beating Andy, I felt the couch move out and a big arm reached over and plucked me out. It was a worse beating than Mother had applied over our previous indiscretion. Thinking back with some maturity and experience with boys of my own, I realize that bad things can happen quite innocently when adults do not provide proper supervision. My parents are lucky that we did not cause something really tragic during those days we were left alone, or the Lord watched over us.

Chapter 2

Primary and Elementary Learning

Andy goes to school

Dad did not want his children playing in kindergarten. He believed formal serious schooling should start at around seven years old. Andy turned seven in the summer of 1946 and started first grade that fall. Upon his return from the first day of school, he told me he had made a couple of friends, so the day was not wasted. In the following days, he brought home number papers, printed practice sheets, and what today would be called language arts exercises involving compound words and similar worksheets. Reading started simple, "Look, Jane, look." "See the dog run." Soon Andy brought home more meaningful books about American historical figures. He was a good reader and had me pretty well through first grade before I got there.

Andy (left) and I on the front stoop of the big house. Notice pants cuff. New overalls were purchased oversize to allow for lots of shrinkage and a child's growth.

Without Andy home, I spent much more time with Mother. We baked cookies, made bread, canned fruit and vegetables, ran the sewing machine, fed clothes through the washing machine wringer, ironed my sisters' dresses (no permanent press back then), swept and mopped floors, went shopping in town or Cortland, and listened to the radio soap operas. I learned the techniques of boiling and frying food on the stove top. She also visited aunts for gab sessions and attended Home Bureau meetings for farmers' wives. All men should have the housekeeping skills I picked up from her during that year.

Lee R. Clendenning, PhD

Beginning trade training

In 1947, Dad decided I should begin my trade training with a project which covered two years of off and on work. The decision was made to convert an old fashioned, walk-through country pantry in one corner of the house into a modern, compact kitchen. Raised work counters, stainless steel surfaces, upper cabinets and a pass-through service window between the kitchen and dining areas were the newest ideas. I first helped him wreck the old floor to ceiling cupboards and throw the debris down into the cellar for burning in the furnace. We then built work counters on the sides of the room with rough lumber from the forest and installed a double basin sink connected to our first electric water heater.

A child helper was expected to keep his attention on the work in progress without symptoms of attention deficit disorder. I had to know the tools by name, hand tools to Dad when he asked for them, go after tools as needed, and learn by observation and trial and error. We built an upper set of what passed for cabinet shelves with sliding plywood doors. Dad's pride was a set of tilt out bins that each held at least 50 pounds of flour, sugar, and salt. In place of stainless steel, Dad found some sheet metal roofing material. This material had ripples manufactured into it along the edges for joining one piece to the next. It became my task to pound out these ripples with a wooden mallet until they were smooth enough to use as covering for the counter top work surfaces. This metal was also used to line Dad's bins to make them mice and rat proof. With the addition of a small electric range and paint on any wood surfaces that were still visible, the kitchen was complete. A picture of the kitchen would not have been published in *Better Homes and Gardens*, but Dad was proud of it. I can only imagine what my secretly perfectionist Mother really thought. She used that kitchen until I, as a teenager with more formal training behind me, replaced the roofing metal surfaces with modern plastic laminate.

"Pride goes before a fall"

Later that spring, Dad was painting the metal roof on the big barn. It was a classic New England structure, 30' X 60' on the foundation and tall enough to hold lots of hay over a double-row animal stable. The eaves on the road side were over 30 feet high. But, there had been a "lean to" addition built on the back side which lowered the eave line there to around ten feet. Also, on the back side were brush, berry bushes, and briars that would have made a comfortable home for Bre'r Rabbit. Sylvia, Andy, and I climbed up to the barn peak and were scurrying along the ridge like squirrels. Instead of telling us to get off the roof, as any other responsible parent would have done, Dad said, "You kids be careful because if you start slipping, you will not be able to stop yourselves."

Sylvia, with a know it all air, replied, "I can stop myself anytime I want to." With such confidence from my older sister, I said, "Yeah, so can I." She promptly sat down and started herself sliding. I followed right behind her. Luckily, we were on the backside of the ridge. To our alarm and then horror, we discovered that Dad was right! Sylvia landed in the brush with me right on top of her. We were scratched up but not seriously hurt. We went to the house crying for comfort and first aid from Mother. Dad didn't even come off the roof to check on us. The event amused him. For years after, he would look at Sylvia and say tauntingly, "I can stop myself any time I want to." Turning to me he would say, "Yeah, so can I." Then he would chuckle at our expense. Ever since the experience, I have never been so sure that I was in control of my life. As a teenager, this realization kept me from some risky adventures and from yielding to temptations that had the potential of leading to bad consequences.

1947-1948, I Go to School

In the fall of 1947, I started first grade in the red brick building now renovated as the Genevieve P. Staley Civic Center. That same year, Mother started working as a cook in the school cafeteria. She rode the school bus to and from work, so there was no parting trauma on the part of either of us. There were forty-seven other students in my class, more than any teacher should be asked to teach at one time. The overloaded teacher struggled for six weeks until the school administration relieved her by dividing the class. I was among those reassigned to an older teacher, an established member of the community.

In addition to teaching us the three R's, which I already had under control, my new teacher attempted to develop our personal hygiene habits and social skills. Each day, we were to mark on charts if we brushed our teeth, carried a handkerchief, and combed our hair. With this method, she probably encouraged more deception than health. We had to take civilizing social walks around the schoolyard while holding the hand of a member of the opposite sex. She was also big on folk dances and games like A-Tisket, A-Tasket, where different genders chased each other around a circle of students. The big valentine box the teacher prepared was also part of the socialization scheme. I stuffed the box with handmade valentines all addressed to this one girl who did not ever acknowledge my presence. After overhearing Dad's often repeated rants about dancing to my older sisters, I was careful never to mention social activities at home.

I looked forward to my first summer vacation. It was a mixture of increased work responsibilities and genuine fun. Andy and I were assigned more chores for care of the cattle, chickens, and pigs. We went into the pasture mornings and evenings to herd the cows to the barn for milking. We learned to repair wire fences. We were also assigned the summer long task of hand-cutting grass growing under what seemed like miles of electrical fence. Cutting was necessary to prevent the grass from shorting out the available electric shock which kept the animals in the pasture. We enjoyed jumping in the hay to pack it down as the older family clan brought it in.

First Job, Picking Beans with Migrant Workers

To earn some money, Andy and I picked beans and other vegetables for a local commercial grower. When the crop was heavy, the grower would bring in migrant workers to handle the harvest. Among them were the first black people we had ever seen. They were very polite to us as we worked with them. We were paid by the weight of what we picked. When I started, I ate about as fast as I picked, so not much went into the bag. Then I discovered a gas station not too far from the field where they sold a non-carbonated orange soft drink for seven cents a bottle. I could get two cents back when the bottle was returned. Since I could cash out as many times a day as I desired, and since I had no adult supervision, and since the sun was always hot, I would pick until I had enough for a soft drink, take a break, and then repeat the process. We were usually paid half a cent per pound picked, so I picked in fifteen to twenty pound cycles. Needless to say, by the end of the harvest season I had very little to show for my efforts. Andy was much more disciplined. By harvest end he had bought a headlight, a tail light, handle-bar grips, and a speedometer for his bike. This began my economic education.

"Fire! The barn is burning!"

One night in August, I was sleeping on the outside porch veranda in an effort to keep cool. There was always a conflict between the desire to be cool and the desire to avoid the mosquitoes. That night, coolness had won. I was awakened in the wee hours of the morning by Dawn's screams. She had just gotten home from a babysitting job. Her bedroom was on the side of the house facing the barn. Leaning over the veranda railing, I could see flames escaping in the middle peak of the barn roof. We all rushed outside while Mother called the De Ruyter Volunteer Fire Department. Dad went in the barn stable to double check that all the animals were out to pasture.

After the volunteer firemen arrived and started spraying water, I went back to the veranda and watched the progress of the fire. The big barn doors fell off revealing the family car parked within. Each corner of the car sagged as the tires blew one by one. When it became too hot to stay on the open porch, I retreated into the house. It then occurred to me that the house was in danger also. I started praying earnestly that God would somehow spare the house. The heat was intense enough to scorch paint on some of the clapboards and to crack a big glass window in the parlor under Dawn's bedroom, but our house did not burst into flames. I still thank God for that. Knowing there was no hope for the barn, the firemen did their best to minimize damage by putting out spreading fires on other buildings.

By daylight, everything except the barn was under control. The barn was left to burn itself out, which would make clean up safer and easier. I remembered that there was a partial case of dynamite stored in the lean-to structure attached to the main barn. I wondered why it had not exploded. I went back to where I could see what was left of that area. It was all hot ashes. I said to a bystander, "Dad had some dynamite right over there." Dad happened to be within hearing. He angrily dragged me with one hand over my mouth into the Ice Shed. "Don't you say one more word about that dynamite to anybody!"

"Why didn't it explode?" I bravely asked.

Dad calmed down and explained that dynamite will burn in an open fire without exploding if it is not disturbed while burning. He further explained, "I was the first man at the nozzle of the fire hose, and I made sure that we never sprayed the stream in that area."

I said nothing further, but I still had questions which I have never settled. How was he so sure the burning debris falling into the area would not cause a denotation? How could he in good conscience allow his friends and neighbors to be exposed to such danger and remain silent? How many of those volunteers would have stayed to save the rest of our buildings if they had known about the danger? With 120 acres at his disposal, why had Dad not complied with the law and stored his dynamite in a separate remote location with proper warning signs? Why did he not learn from the previous disaster with stored gunpowder? Dad took a horrible gamble. I have concluded that it was indefensible to expose others without their knowledge!

Immediately after the fire, Dad installed cow stanchions in a small barn on the Foster property to provide for milking and housing the cattle during the next winter. With the $1,000 insurance settlement, Dad bought an old Chevy pick-up truck for family transportation, and Mother obtained a new food freezer. I was traumatized enough to pray every night for a long time that there would be no more fires. There weren't any.

1948-1949, Moved from second to third grade

For me, second grade resulted in the first serious life affecting decision. It only lasted the first ten week quarter. My teacher, Mrs. Lee, was a mature lady who had taught all of my older siblings. She was also the wife of the President of the Board of Education. I had read all the books on the classroom shelf. Time hung heavy on my hands. I don't remember what sort of mischief sentenced me to time out in the big coat closet at the rear of the room. There I discovered an old soda-water fire extinguisher which would spray what looked to me like plain water when it was tipped to one side. Thinking it would dry before anybody noticed, I sprayed a little water on the wall and on the backs of a couple of coats. I was allowed to return to the class after a brief period. When it came time to go home, a couple of little girls asked the teacher, "What is this white stuff on our coats?" The water had dried as I had planned, but it left behind the no longer dissolved baking soda. It didn't take Mrs. Lee long to get a confession out of me. No real harm was done, but it was a learning experience for me. Education is sometimes painful.

Another day, my boredom after finishing worksheets led to the life-changing decision. Mrs. Lee asked me why I wasn't as well behaved as Andy. She reported that when he finished his work, he quietly read a book. I replied that I had read them all. After picking a few books at random from the shelf and quizzing me about their various contents, she said, "I will be back in a minute." She went to the library/teacher's smoking room and returned with three books. I described the contents of each. I do not know who talked to whom, but by the following Monday morning, Mrs. Lee's problem was solved. The Principal came to the classroom door, asked for me, and led me over to the third grade classroom. Opening the door, he told the startled teacher that I was now a member of her class. There were 47 students already in that room. Somebody went down to the cafeteria and told my mother. Apparently, Mother had no objections. The only unhappy person was Andy. He didn't see why I could skip a grade when he couldn't.

Academically, and socially, I gained a year. Only the Master Planner could have predicted how critical that year would be in the timing of other events in my life. There was an immediate positive effect on my school performance, and a better match between my early maturing responsibilities and required time to graduate from high school. The gift of a year even made a significant difference in the courtship of my wife, Patricia. Although we were the same age, Patricia was now only one grade ahead of me in a different school. She had started first grade at five years old. There is a small likelihood that a serious friendship would have blossomed between a rising female sophomore and a boy in eighth grade.

It appeared that my third grade teacher really did not like children. She was a rugged woman with a big strong hand. If she thought one of us boys were misbehaving, she would grab the culprit by the back of the neck, squeeze her thumb and index finger together until one thought his head would pop off, lift the student up on his toes, and march him out of the room. After experiencing this treatment, it was not a process that I wanted repeated.

That Christmas season, every class had to take part in an all school assembly program in the high school auditorium. To represent the third grade, the teacher asked me to recite the complete poem, *The Night Before Christmas,* as our only contribution. The recitation went well, but I have often wondered why I, as a late comer, was chosen over the other children, or why an activity involving more children was not planned. This event, coupled with short parts in church Christmas and Easter programs started my training in public speaking.

Barn wrecking and remodeling

In the spring of my third grade, our neighbor's big barn started collapsing. Dad made a deal with the neighbor to tear down the barn and clean up the site in exchange for the material. The barn was 40' by 120', more than double the size of our burned one. So every spare minute was spent climbing over the structure prying up boards and pulling what seemed like thousands of nails. Although the work was real drudgery, I learned a lot about taking things apart while minimizing real damage. When enough material had been collected, Dad had a series of work bees in which extended family members helped us modify what had been a horse barn into a stable suitable for a small dairy. By fall, the barn was full of hay, and the cows were moved into the remodeled building. I did learn a lot about concrete, structure, tool use, and teamwork.

A private space of our own

About this time, my sisters wanted more privacy in their sleeping quarters. The upstairs of the homestead had never been finished properly into private rooms. In fact, Mother and Dad's bedroom was the only one with a door. It was decided that Andy and I would make a bedroom on the back side of the house in a lean-to structure between the house and the woodshed. This area apparently had been built as an external laundry room. The space was enclosed on three sides. The fourth side had a wide doorway opening to the walkway to the woodshed and also leading to the outside world. There was a pair of uncased twin windows on the west wall and some attic space above. During the summer, it seemed like a good idea, kind of like camping out, mosquitoes and all. As the weather got colder, Mother got feather mattresses out of the attic, and we pushed our single beds together to create a double one to share body heat. When the west wind lightly drifted snow through the unfinished windows, she found old waterproof bear coats to cover our blankets. The barn cats soon learned where we were. They would come in, and we would let them sleep under the blankets for warmth. The only drawback was that they would occasionally wake us up as they demanded entry or came out for air. After the neighbor's Great Dane and a skunk visited us, I found doors somewhere and shut out the animals. The lean-to was our own territory for five years until all the sisters left home.

Chapter 3

My Family Changes Churches

About this time, my parents became dissatisfied with the local church in De Ruyter. It was a community Federated Church with people from Baptist, Methodist, and Congregational groups whose individual churches in the community had closed sometime in the past. I was too young to pay attention to sermons, but from listening to my parents, I understood that the Pastor was using the Revised Version of the Bible and had publically questioned such traditional elements of faith as the virgin birth, the real existence of Hell, the accuracy of scripture, and whether Jesus was the only way to heaven. By some, his theological teachings were called "Going Modern." The majority of the congregation was apparently not unhappy with the trend. I do not recall being taught in that church that one must be saved or born again. The blood of Jesus was never mentioned. I do not recall a Communion service. I remember their singing *Holy, Holy, Holy* each Sunday and *In the Garden* or *What a Friend We have in Jesus* quite often. One could conclude that God loved us and that good people were going to heaven after death. I also do not remember hearing about the Devil and Hell in church.

Beyond overheard grumbling, I do not know what communication the adults may have had with former friends. One day, a holiness preacher from Lower Cincinnatus, twenty-three miles away, showed up in our yard. He wanted Dawn to play piano for his church services.

The following Sunday, the whole family, including Dad, loaded into the car and went to his church. It was an eye-opening experience for me.

First of all, everyone seemed to know Mother and Dad; apparently my Grandfather Perry had preached there in years gone by. They seemed pleased to meet us children and counted us carefully. Next was the singing. They "raised the rafters" in volume, if not in tunefulness. At the time for Morning Prayer, a "Prayer Leader" was designated. Most everyone turned around and knelt using his or her chair as an altar while praying not quite as loudly as the leader. They all seemed to sense when the leader was about finished, and they were polite enough to finish ahead of him (or her) so that prayer was clearly over when the leader finished. When I got used to the idea, I figured the Lord could sort it all out. Then the preaching—VERY LOUD!—all about needing to be saved in order to avoid Hell. I now understood Dad's remarks about sleeping in the more tame services. I learned later that this style was called preaching "Hellfire and Brimstone". In subsequent services, Hell was so vividly described that I could almost smell the smoke. I now know that it was intended to scare the Hell out of me. The process started that day.

We went back for the evening service which was similar to the morning one except a time was set aside for personal testimonies, the first ones I remember hearing. People were very happy to be "saved" and "sanctified holy," new concepts for me. A former alcoholic explained that when he was saved, he became a new creature; old desires and habits passed away and all things became new. A man described how an old accident had left him with a deformed neck. He had walked for years with his head tilted to one side. Now, he stood straight and tall. He said that when Jesus saves a man, he stands him straight up! In succeeding services, I witnessed what I learned was called divine healing. The person seeking healing was anointed with oil and the older people gathered around in a circle, touching the seeker with their hands while they prayed. These people believed that God, Jesus, the Holy Spirit, Heaven, the Devil, and Hell were all very real. They believed that God did hear their prayers and occasionally answered in miraculous ways. They believed that the people of the world were lost and headed for Hell if someone didn't share the Gospel with them.

They supported missions and had missionaries from exotic places come and describe their work. In time, this church gave me a whole new theological outlook to consider and a new vocabulary to describe the experiences.

The church building was a small blacksmith shop converted for services and heated by a big pot-bellied stove in one corner. The preaching platform in front was separated by an altar for kneeling in prayer. The congregation was usually twenty-five to thirty people; forty was a crowd! There were a couple of families bigger than ours. There were also older grandmothers, grandfathers, and widows. The preacher worked for a railroad through the week. The church was affiliated with a small conference of similar churches scattered widely in New York State and Ohio. The Conference sponsored youth camps and old-fashioned adult camp meetings each summer near Binghamton, New York. We worshiped at that church until I was twelve years old.

First baptism by immersion

Sometime during the summer of 1949, Dad decided that he should be baptized. Typical of him, he also thought what was good for him would also be good for the rest of us. So one Sunday afternoon, the Church sponsored a baptismal service at Cincinnatus Lake, which was actually south of the Village of Willet, New York. Dad lined us all up by age, and we were immersed one at a time. I went in the water a dry sinner and came up a wet one, with no idea what it was all about. I never discussed the event with my brother or sisters, so I do not know how much they understood.

". . . whoever calls on the name of the Lord shall be saved . . ." (Joel 2:32)

As time passed, I became very convinced that I was a sinner headed for Hell unless I was saved. When altar calls were given, I would go forward, kneel and pray, "God save me." Others would gather around me and pray for me. Their testimonies described tears of repentance, so I tried crying. Their testimonies described "taking time to pray through," so I tried staying at the altar until everyone but my family left for home. If people really explained the concept of Jesus paying the price for my sins, it went over my head. I heard them sing *Amazing Grace*, and *God's Grace*, which was greater than all my sins. However, I had no working concept of what grace was or how it applied to me. I don't understand why I was slow to comprehend the message because it was in their music, if nowhere else. Was I saved? Maybe so if I claimed the promise that "whoever calls." I did repent of my many sins, many times. I understood the judgment of God, but not the real love of God. I certainly did not feel saved. I finally decided to act as if I was saved anyway and hope for the best. This went on until my realization of salvation at Delta Lake summer camp when I was thirteen years old.

Chapter 4

Living and Learning— Middle Grades and Junior High

Fourth grade

I started fourth grade in the fall of 1949. The teacher was relatively new to the system and certainly "not from around here." Her husband was the physical education teacher and coach at the high school. She apparently liked music. But, as was the case throughout my years in public education, my life centered on making a living rather than schooling.

I launch the chicken business

At nine years old, I started seriously studying the chicken business, and chickens became my primary means of support for a number of years. For our immediate family needs, we had been depending on setting hens for eight to a dozen new chicks each summer. I subscribed to *Everybody's Poultry Magazine* and read it faithfully each month. I plotted and schemed how I could make money raising broilers and selling them. I calculated such things as the cost of mail order chicks, the amount of feed per bird needed for it to reach market size, and the maximum growing time. I showed my figures to Dad and to my sister Ruth. Ruth was the "banker" among us children. Ruth loaned me $8.00 to order 100 Rhode Island Red chicks. Dad bought a used baby chick brooder capable of serving 100 chicks. I cleaned out an old brooder house that had not been used for years, and I was in business.

After the chicks came by postal delivery, I was so excited that I almost individually nurtured them for a few days. Then one morning I went out to find only about twenty-five of them in the brooder house. I saw no sign of the others, nor any clue as to what had happened to them. I reported the situation to Dad. After checking my facts and discovering a hole chewed between two side boards low in the brooder house wall, he announced that it was the work of a rat. He told me to get the shotgun while he went after the tractor. The brooder house was built on a foundation of wood skids like modern backyard storage buildings. He hitched the tractor to a skid and pulled the building back about twenty feet. Sure enough, there were my 75 dead chicks littered around the rat's straw nest. Dad took the shotgun, kicked the nest, and shot the rat when it ran for safety.

I asked Dad why the rat killed so many when it couldn't possibly have eaten all those chicks. He explained that the rat liked blood, so he grabbed a chick, took it to his home under the building, sucked a little blood, and then went back for another. He told me to bury the dead chicks and then nail roofing metal around the bottom two feet of the brooder house walls. This would prevent more rats from getting the rest of the chicks. I now understood why the floor of the brooder house was already covered with sheet metal.

The rat incident was really a long-term blessing. Not having a mass of chickens to slaughter, I shifted plans and raised the remaining hens into layers. The family ate the roosters. Ruth must have felt sorry for me because she never mentioned the $8.00 loan. By the following school year, I was selling eggs to the local Red and White grocery store. In subsequent seasons, I made good use of the brooder, ordering batches of chicks and feeding them until they were big enough to sell. Selling them alive to a dealer was the easiest path. A few times, I dressed a batch of them to sell on the fresh meat market, although I did not enjoy picking all the feathers and the other dressing tasks. I became financially independent from then on, buying my own clothes, tools, toys, and school lunches.

Summer of 1950—more trade training

During the summer of 1950, I continued my trade training interspersed around the farm work. Dad volunteered to install a new roof on the parsonage of the church we were attending. Many in the family went with him to tear off the old roofing, repair and replace roof boards, and then put on new asphalt shingles. I learned to use a chalk line to keep shingles straight, to position and nail down new shingles, and to stick down the loose tabs of the shingles with tar to keep them from blowing off in a storm. I got lots of tar on me!

When the church job was over, Uncle Lewis Hanes hired me to do the same thing on our former Little House which was now his. He was afraid of heights, but he would climb the ladder just enough to stick his head over the eaves and check on my progress. I was proud to have completed the job all by myself!

After the roof job for Uncle Louis, Dad moved me into installation of asbestos siding. A traveling salesman had sold Dad on the idea of covering the house with asbestos siding to ward off future fires. Dad made a home-built table saw to cut the shingles, and I was assigned to help. The shingles should have been cut with a guillotine knife which created practically no dust. But, Dad's saw created a cloud of dust too thick to see through every time it was used. Other family members worked with us some of the time. The house was mostly covered, but to my knowledge, the job was never really completed. I think of this experience when I see lawyer's advertisements for mesothelioma cases on TV.

Dad also decided that I should learn how to put casings on windows. Neither the windows upstairs nor those on the side porch built years before by Grandma Clendenning had ever been cased on the inside. Our lumber was all rough hemlock from our forests, just as it came from the saw mill. None of the wood was standard sized. Dad took scarce money and purchased a portable electric saw and a jointer-planer. The portable saw was a powerful, heavy, monstrous ancestor to the modern, light skill saw. I did not know until years later that the jointer-planer was considered the most dangerous machine in a school woodshop. I learned to master both machines to cut the material to size and smooth the surfaces to accept paint. I cased the porch windows and installed a screened storm door.

Machinery operators

During the transition from horse power to tractors, haying equipment was still designed for horses. With horses, one person could ride and operate the equipment while simultaneously driving the horses. A tractor pulling the same equipment required a separated driver and operator. Andy and I worked for neighbors as equipment operators behind their tractors. Eventually, we graduated to a Ford 8N tractor with rubber tires. Andy became an excellent tractor driver. He could work the machine to capacity on steep hillsides and in the woods. Eventually, Dad purchased a rear mounted, hydraulically operated mower which could be operated by a single person. Andy and I took turns mowing hay for neighbors.

Fifth grade

For fifth grade, we moved from the old red brick school to the high school building on the west end of town. The class was divided into two different home rooms. My group felt lucky because we drew one of the most respected teachers in the system, Mrs. Mildred Blowers (who later married a man named Parker). Her reputation for excellence was verified as the year progressed. She divided the class into two competitive groups named after birds, the "Blue Jays" and the "Robins," as I remember it. We spent some of our time tutoring the slower kids in our group in spelling and arithmetic. Fridays were quiz days. Each group tried to make its bird fly higher on the graphic score board she designed.

In fifth grade, we left the classroom for physical education in place of recess. The physical education class separated the boys and girls for the first time. The high school coach required us to change into uniforms and take showers, which we thought were fun. Students were expected to pay for their uniforms, but the coach said that if anyone "had a problem with that," he would give him a uniform. Neither Andy nor I had been prepared to pay that day, so we innocently told him that we didn't have any money. He issued us the uniforms. Somehow Dad found out about our action, and he was very angry. "We are not charity cases or on welfare!" he stormed. "You boys go in there tomorrow and pay that coach his money!" It was the first time I had ever heard that there was such a thing as welfare for poor people. We paid the coach.

Peer influence

In fifth grade, I also had an unfortunate experience with peer influence. The high school junior class was allowed to operate a concession stand each noon hour to raise money for their senior trip. Being now financially independent, I got into the habit of buying a couple of candy bars and sharing the second one with one of my neighbor kids. In the winter, I started playing Jacks on the floor with one of the girls who was new that year. I gave her the extra candy bar. Before long, some of the other boys noticed what was going on. They started teasing me and telling me that the only reason she would play with me was to get the candy. Like a fool, I started believing them. I will always remember the bewildered and hurt look on her face when I told her I wouldn't play with her anymore. Later, I realized she had been an innocent victim of my peer's jealously, and I felt bad. However, I never explained my actions to her. She moved away the following year. Since then, I have been wary of peer pressure.

Sixth Grade—formal English rejected

I started sixth grade with a group of unhappy classmates in the fall of 1951. The grade was still split into two classes, and our group felt cheated because the excellent teacher we were expecting was reassigned as a reading specialist. The new teacher was older and from outside the community. She tried to introduce us to nouns, verbs, subjects, predicates, and other rules for formal grammar and proper sentence structures, but at the time, "us farm boys" didn't appreciate the value of such concepts. Looking back, I see that she worked hard to overcome the starting handicap.

The "Tin Top" gospel meetings

During the previous summer, Mr. Robert (Bob) Rowe, a new owner of the Red and White grocery store, started talking to my folks about bringing the gospel to town. He had connections to an evangelist willing to come for a series of meetings for just his room, board, and a free will offering. Arrangements were made to use The Tin Top as a meeting place. The Tin Top was a local dance hall (which my parents would not normally have entered) on top of the hill bordering the south side of the village. It was a big Quonset structure with a totally metal exterior (hence the name, "Tin Top") enclosing a large smooth wood floor. A local funeral home loaned chairs which were set up on the dance floor. The evangelist with his wife and a twelve-year-old son were scheduled to stay with us for a week in the fall. It was unseasonably cold and rainy that week, even by New York standards. Being from North Carolina, the Preacher and his family thought they were going to freeze to death. We built a fire in the basement furnace which supplied heat to one large living room register above it, but our farm house did not have a central air circulation system at the time. Each night of the meetings, we had to arrive well before the scheduled time in order to start the building heater. Andy and I were not accustomed to that much interior free space. Mother allowed us to play tag around the seating area until the first guests arrived. The meetings were sparsely attended.

On Saturday of the same week, Andy and I were "shocking" corn. This was the process of manually standing bundles of corn stalks on end around a "corn horse." The corn horse was a modified saw horse with a removable cross rod which held up stalks leaned against it until enough were placed to form the familiar self-standing cone shape. The corn horse was then removed to be used again in forming the next corn shock. The stored corn was used for animal feed during the coming winter.

On a pleasant day, shocking corn was fun. Andy and I often made imaginary games or simple physical contests out of our work. On a nice day, we might have been making a whole Indian village of tee pees, but shocking corn was miserable work on a cold rainy day. We were too macho to share our imaginations with a total stranger. Not understanding what was really going on, the Preacher's wife sent her son out to "play" with us. It was obvious he had never worked a day in his life. Before long, he was in tears and returned to the house to beg his mother to let him stay there. She may have thought we were not very sociable. In fairness to him, that evening he showed us big blisters on the bottom of one foot.

My future wife

Saturday night of the meetings, the first guests to arrive were a family we did not know. With the parents were a girl near my age, a younger brother, and a sister in her mother's arms. Andy and I had plenty of time to study the family before the service actually started. The mother had a stern, no nonsense manner about her. The younger brother had his father's big brown eyes. The girl captured my attention. She was tall for her age. Little did I suspect that someday she would become my wife!

Seventh grade—in shop at last!

I looked forward to seventh grade because boys were required to spend a semester in the school agriculture shop. We had never heard of industrial arts or vocational industrial education. By this point, there was nothing the teacher could teach me about the tools; I just wanted to get my hands on them. I made the required projects: a wooden puzzle and a lamp designed to look like an old fashioned water pump. Then the teacher let me make a small bookcase. I also sharpened tools for him.

4-H (Head, Heart, Health, & Hands)

Our Agriculture teacher was also the 4-H Advisor for the district. He encouraged some of us to start a Junior High 4-H Chapter. To my surprise, Dad let me join, and I was elected Chapter President. We met for the rest of the year during the Friday afternoon activity periods set aside for extracurricular groups. We were taught about leadership skills, parliamentary procedure (how to conduct meetings and record minutes of proceedings), how to conduct home farm projects, and how to make oral reports and presentations. My chicken business provided a natural project. I showed one group of chickens at the New York State Fair. Years later, as a Parliamentarian for the International Industrial Arts Association (among other offices), I went back to the principles taught to seventh graders in 4-H. The Unseen Hand knew what competencies I would need in the future and started building them in me. ("For I know the plans I have for you," declares the Lord, "plans to prosper you and not to harm you, plans to give you hope and a future.") (Jeremiah 29:11 (NIV)

Gospel services begin again

In the spring of 1953, Bob Rowe again approached my folks about starting gospel services in De Ruyter. He had connections to a preacher in training at the Baptist Bible Seminary in Johnson City, NY. Services were scheduled in the local Grange Hall for Sunday evenings. The local Grangers owned a building with meeting rooms upstairs and a deep narrow room downstairs which in the past, had housed a retail store. The meetings were better advertised and attended than those at the old Tin Top. My Aunt Doris Foster, who did not normally attend any church, was recruited to play the piano for singing. In her younger days she had played the piano for the melodrama effects at silent movies.

At one of the early meetings, I recognized the same family of outsiders as the folks with the daughter who had attended the Saturday night service at the Tin Top. I learned that they were the Terrill family from Fabius, a village about eleven miles away. The daughter's name was Patricia. Eleven miles does not seem very far in today's world, but in that region the distance meant a different county, school system, and athletic league, as well as a long distance telephone call. They came from a local Methodist church which had started to propagate more modern ideas. The family's search for a fundamental, evangelical place to worship brought them to De Ruyter. Otherwise, the probability of my becoming acquainted with Patricia and our future courtship and marriage would have been much more unlikely.

Summer of 1953—serious farming

During the summer of 1953, Andy and I started shipping milk to a cheese factory in Taylor, NY. We used dynamite to blast a deep hole in one of the really cold springs. Then I built a wooden rack to hold the milk cans submerged into the water, and that became our refrigeration system. We were milking by hand one squirt at a time and produced enough to meet the needs of our family, calves, and pigs, and still tried to sell about eight to ten gallons every other day.

That summer, Dad also placed the complete responsibility for cutting the winter wood on our shoulders. We had axes and a long crosscut saw to cut down the trees. Andy and I had different natural working speeds. He was quick; I was slow. Eventually he would get impatient with me and saw alone. I became an expert with the axe. I could chop down a tree leaving the stump as smooth as if it had been sawn. We both were sure that if Dad had to do the work, he would buy a chain saw. We used the tractor to drag the logs we cut from the woods to the house area and accumulated them into a huge "Buzz Pile." Late in the fall, often on Thanksgiving Day, a family crew would hold a work bee and cut the wood into standard lengths.

First Visit to the Dentist

Typical dental care was a low priority in the family. I always had a tooth brush somewhere. By twelve-years-old, I had developed one big cavity in a side molar which was sensitive to heat and cold. I complained, and Dad took me to Cortland for my first dental check. The dentist said it should be filled, but Dad told him to pull the tooth to be sure it would never bother again. It hasn't! I didn't visit a dentist again until I was sixteen. Then an accident in the woods broke off a lower front tooth. I had the tooth stump and roots pulled, and that one has never bothered again either.

Eighth Grade

By Christmas and New Years of my eighth grade, on Sundays I started noticing Patricia from Fabius. She occasionally played the piano and/or the accordion for congregational singing. When I tried to attract her attention, she was friendly, but nothing more. At the watch night service, some of us young people were drafted to take turns babysitting with the pastor's young children while he and his wife conducted the meeting. My turn came right after Patricia's at about 10 o'clock. I tried to strike up a conversation, but she felt she had to return to the service immediately. When I was relieved by the next person, I went back to the service. I discovered that Andy had taken a seat on the front row, piano side, tipped his head back, and was fast asleep. There was only one chair open in that row, which was beside him. Patricia had just finished playing and went back quietly and took that seat. I thought, "The lucky dog; and he doesn't know enough to enjoy it!" In the weeks following, I made a couple more attempts to get Patricia's attention, and then I gave up. I figured she would never know I really existed. There was another fellow in the church who was obviously trying to play the same game. He apparently had made no more progress than I had.

A Valentine from Patricia

However, on Valentine's Day, 1954, I got the most pleasant surprise of my life. In the mail was a nice valentine from Patricia. I was shocked! She did know that I existed after all! I was walking on air! Andy had also gotten a card from her that day, but the sentiment expressed wasn't as nice as mine. I never heard him say a word about his card; I was too wrapped up in myself to consider competition from him. Imagine my surprise the next day when my real rival confronted me in the school hall with a valentine card from Patricia identical to mine! He was as excited as I had been. Learning that I also received a card, he demanded to see it. I kept my wits and assured him that my card was much nicer than his. It wasn't a complete lie; my card had my name on it and his did not! He bugged me for days to see my card, but I always "forgot" to bring it to school. I learned much later that Patricia had also sent the same card to a third fellow in a distant church that her family had occasionally visited. At this point in time, for me, "ignorance was bliss."

My rival was a clean cut, all-American boy from a respected family that lived in town. In time, he became a high school athletic star and still later, by all reports, a successful civil engineer. He didn't give up attempting to get Patricia's attention right up to our wedding day. In fact, on that day, he not only failed to come through the reception line to wish us well; he also dumped confetti into my punch so that I could not drink it.

Cultivating a Friendship

In plotting to get better acquainted with Patricia, I decided I could play the "little brother" game. I had experienced fellows pretending to be interested in me while they were really interested in one of my sisters. I invited Patricia's younger brother, Douglas, to spend a Sunday afternoon between church services with me. We had a big country Sunday dinner, knocked around the fields in an old Model A Ford which Andy and I had acquired from a junk yard, did chores, and returned to evening service after a light supper. It worked! Before very long, the invitation to spend Sunday afternoon with Douglas at his home was extended. I rode with his family to the Terrill dairy farm in the edge of the village of Fabius. Doug and I played with his extensive model train system while his mother prepared Sunday dinner. After dinner, Patricia and her little sister, Evelyn, accompanied Doug and me to the home gym in the barn which was setup for basketball. In the course of the afternoon, Doug (and

I think, Patricia) caught on to my real interests. I don't think Doug ever forgave me. He mentioned the event a number of times in later years.

The wangled invitation from Doug was the start of a real friendship with Patricia. I started waiting for her family to arrive on Sunday mornings so that I could carry her accordion into service. After service, I would carry the accordion back to the trunk of the car. There were no more invitations to her house; I had burned the "Little Brother Bridge" behind me. I needed a second plot to spend some time with Patricia outside of a church service or Young Peoples meeting. My opportunity came when I was asked to recite the Gettysburg Address for Memorial Day Services in De Ruyter that year. Memorial Day was on a Sunday, and the cemetery services were scheduled for the afternoon to avoid conflict with churches. Patricia would be playing in the band for the services in Fabius, but they were scheduled for Monday morning. I asked Patricia if she could get permission to spend the afternoon with me in order to hear me speak. To my delight, permission was granted. We enjoyed the usual Sunday dinner, and then Mother took Patricia and me to the services. The rest of my family was not interested in my personal honor. The Address went well; I only faltered once, and a nearby veteran whispered the prompt I needed. One of my classmates made me look even better when she read, (rather than recited) the poem, *In Flanders Field*. After our marriage, I learned from Patricia that she was very favorably impressed by my performance that day. If I had realized at the time how important the event was in establishing our relationship, I would have been much more nervous. She likes to watch people's faces as she tells them that our first date was to the cemetery.

Chapter 5

Summer, 1954—
Salvation Realized!

Delta Lake Youth Camp

During the early summer of 1954, I had a life changing spiritual experience. I decided to attend the same youth camp at Delta Lake near Rome, NY, that I had learned Patricia would be attending. The camp was operated by the Christian and Missionary Alliance. Patricia was to stay as a guest of long-term family friends who owned a cabin right on the camp grounds. The camp was scheduled just after haying but before grain harvest, which was perfect for me. I decided I was going as a regular camper.

I instinctively knew there would be some resistance to my plan. Dad had to be convinced that I could be gone a week. The year before, he vetoed my attendance at the youth camp sponsored by our former holiness group because work needed to be done. Andy said he could handle chores without me, so Dad agreed to let me go. I only needed the cooperation of Patricia's parents in providing transportation. Although I am not naturally a pushy individual, this time I deliberately pushed in where I knew I wouldn't be welcomed. (One of my philosophies of life is that it is often easier to obtain forgiveness than permission.) I decided that rather than ask permission, I would tell them what I was going to do, and see if they would block it. I told them that I was going to go to youth camp, but I needed to ride out and back with them when they took Patricia. Her mother made it very plain that if I went, I could not stay as a guest of their friends. That was fine with me.

The camp was well-staffed and well-organized. I stayed in a tent village with three other boys in my tent. Boys were expected to keep their living quarters clean and neat. When we didn't win the neatness prize the first day because my city dwelling tent mates didn't know how to make a bed, I told them to forget about it and stay out of the way. I kept house (or tent) after that, and we won the neatness prize four of the remaining days.

I enjoyed the camp schedule. The early morning swim in the crystal clear lake at 6:00 a.m. was a real treat. I usually had to get up well before that time. Everybody gathered around the flag pole for the Pledge of Allegiance and prayer to start the official day, followed by breakfast, a free period, and then a missionary story. Our assigned missionary had served in the wilds of Borneo. After another break, there was the Bible lesson. After lunch, there were team sport competitions and swimming. After supper, there was an evangelical evening service, often attended by additional adults who apparently drove in from local areas. I carried Patricia's accordion back and forth to the Tabernacle so that she could play with the band for the group singing.

The realization of salvation

Bible study was the eye opener for me. Our teacher started with the verse in Hebrews 9:22, "Without the shedding of blood there is no remission of sin." Then he turned to God's shedding the blood of animals to cover the sin of Adam and Eve, and traced the idea of a blood sacrifice throughout the Bible. This concept culminated in Jesus shedding His blood for us on the cross. Parallel to this line of history and thought was the motivation of God to express His love for us. Romans 5:8 says, "God commendeth His love for us in that while we were yet sinners, Christ died for us." God's grace was defined as "unmerited favor." At some point, the truths of the scriptures I had heard many times before suddenly became meaningful. I saw the Light! Even though I didn't deserve it, God loved ME! Christ paid the penalty for MY sins! Like the travelers on the road to Emmaus (Luke 24:13-25), my heart burned within me for three days as I soaked the truths of His Word into my soul. Being "saved" meant more than a fire escape from Hell. I needed to do more than simply call "Lord save me." Being a follower of Jesus went beyond the simple repentance of feeling sorry for my sin to a commitment to seek His will and do it for the rest of my life. We were challenged by Romans 12:1: "I beseech you therefore brethren, by the mercies of God. That you present your bodies a living sacrifice, holy, acceptable unto God, which is your reasonable service." Many of us sang, "I'll go where you want me to go, Dear Lord," with tears in our eyes and real commitment in our hearts. Being "born again" was an answer to my and David's prayers: "Create in me a clean heart, O God; and renew a right spirit within me" (Psalm 51:10). My life was drastically changed for the better that week. I now understand the source of my courage to be "pushy" to get to summer camp. God had a Divine appointment with me! From then on I have been able to shake off many old inhibitions, openly sing the praises of our Lord, and share my faith with those interested.

The Birth of Little Brother Dan

Also in the summer of 1954, the birth of my brother Dan caused Dad to revaluate his need for God. There was a maternity home in De Ruyter, complete with midwife and a competent doctor on call, but Dad saw no need of the facilities. A home birth appeared to be an easy decision for Dad since he had never personally experienced a really difficult delivery. My older sister, Ruth, who had nursing training, was drafted to assist the doctor. Mother was forty-four years old, and Dan was big. After a long hard delivery, I was finally allowed into the room to see Mother and my new brother. Baby Daniel was fine, but Mother was too weak to talk and blue-gray in complexion. To me, it was very apparent that her survival was in question. I found a place of prayer. I understand from later remarks that this was the night that Dad trusted Jesus as his savior as he pleaded before God for his wife's life. I also understand that Mother also pleaded with God for the opportunity to care for her son. Praise the Lord for her recovery!

Chapter 6

Going Steady for Years—Early Ministry

After Delta Lake Summer Camp, Patricia and I were as much of a couple as our youth and the expectations of our parents and the culture would allow. We were too young to drive, so we had to depend on our parents and the Pastor for transportation. Dad always had to be reimbursed for gas, or car service, or both. A grease job and change of oil seemed to be needed quite often when I needed someone to drive me to De Ruyter or Fabius. Dad was never the chauffeur, so Mother or an older sister was usually drafted.

The Pastor would load a car full of kids into his old Plymouth on Saturday nights and take us to Cortland Christian Youth Time. These meetings were held in the Courthouse Auditorium about twenty miles away, further if he went by way of Fabius to allow Patricia to join us. I was amused by the rules and logic of the adults. They could pile us three deep into the car going to or from an event, but while we were there, the genders were to keep respectable distances from each other. The only exception was at an annual roller skating party also sponsored by Youth for Christ. There, we followed the routines the management enforced. Patricia was a good skater and used her own skates. I enjoyed the "Couples Only" moonlight skates which always ended the evening. Dates to movies and dances, even those sponsored by our different schools, were "No No's!" to both sets of parents.

About this time, Patricia's mother suddenly decided that her whole family should sit together in church services. Maybe someone noticed that we were holding hands under Patricia's big Bible as we followed the sermon's text references. Patricia's mother pointedly chose a row with only five chairs in it, leaving no room for me. So, I chose to sit directly behind Patricia, letting her know I was there in subtle ways. We submitted to this seating arrangement through courtship, engagement, and until marriage.

Throughout the rest of our high school years, Patricia and I took leadership roles in the newly formed church youth group. There was no adult direction or leadership, so we took turns planning programs for our Sunday night meetings ahead of the evening service. I even led the group singing choruses while Patricia played the piano or accordion. We planned seasonal activities such as picnics, Halloween parties, Christmas caroling, and moonlight snow sliding. There was no shortage of high hills or snow in Fabius or in my farm area. Our Sunday meetings were sparsely attended, but kids came out of the woodwork for a party, especially if we did all the planning and supplied all the food. We did have a time of devotion at each event through which they patiently suffered.

Setting up an early evening treasure hunt and picnic at Highland Park was typical of our different personalities and approaches to our work. This public park was on the edge of a State Forest Preserve on a big hill about four miles outside of Fabius. Patricia and I planned a private bicycle outing earlier in the day to go there, reserve a picnic area, hide the ultimate treasure, and fasten clues to trees. I begged a ride to Fabius that morning. We prepared the clues along with a light lunch. Patricia was to ride her bicycle while I was to use her brother's bike. I was envisioning a leisurely ride with pleasant conversation through the beautiful countryside. Sounds like fun, doesn't it?

As we started pedaling up through the village of Fabius, I realized I was in trouble. Doug's bike apparently had never been lubricated. The chain was stiff. Worse yet, one tire was rubbing against the frame acting as a perpetual brake. Patricia took off up the street as if it were a Tour de France race, never glancing back. Looking ahead, I could see her hunched over the handle bars lifting up one foot while she put down the other. She was very soon out of calling range. I struggled along, eventually out of breath, but too proud to quit or go back for repairs.

We continued this way for three miles. Luckily for me, Highland Forest Hill was too steep to pedal up on an old bicycle without a modern gear shifter. I caught Patricia part way up the hill, and we pushed the bikes the rest of the way up. Setting up the hunt and the lunch went fine. Going home was a repeat performance. When Patricia has a task to do, she gets it done! Our picnic and hunt that evening was a great success. Years later, her focused energy and work ethic was what provided the help I needed for success in my academic career.

Patricia and I communicated between Sundays largely through letters. A first class stamp was only three cents. A long distance telephone call to Fabius was fifteen cents for the first three minutes. When I needed to talk to Patricia immediately, I would pay Dad the dime and nickel. He would time me to be sure I didn't talk too long. So much for a private conversation! The phone offered no privacy anyway because our rural party line had ten to fifteen households connected at any given time. Any one of them could pick up the receiver and listen to any conversation taking place. As more people listened in, the voice message one heard became weaker. When Dad used the phone, he would say, "If some of you old biddies would hang up, I would be able to hear my party." Letters took two days at the most depending on the time of day they were mailed. All through high school, I did spend time during classes writing to my sweetheart, which was not as much of a distraction as today's students swapping immediate text messages.

Chapter 7

Beginning High School

In the fall of 1954, upon entering high school I was forced to plan my academic program for the next four years. There were only two main choices, College Prep or General/Vocational. The general/vocational area had further choices of Home Economics, Vocational Agriculture, or Business. Andy and his friends entered the Vo Ag program. I was already operating the farm with him, and I had participated in 4-H for two years. With the arrogance of the ignorant, I didn't think I would learn much more in Vo Ag. I chose the College Prep, but refused to take the required French or Latin, neither of which interested me. When told that I couldn't go to college without a foreign language, I insisted that I was **_never_** going to college anyway. I filled out my schedule with Mechanical Drafting which was offered by the Art Department. This course sounded interesting to me because I wanted to learn how to make and read blue prints of structural plans. After completing the first year of mechanical drafting, the principal allowed me to continue advanced independent studies in the field under his supervision. My parents didn't care what I studied, or if I studied. The Unseen Hand was working here because it turned out later when I did apply to Oswego State Teachers College to become an Industrial Arts teacher, I would not have been admitted without the mechanical drawing courses, or the other College Prep classes I did take.

Andy Forced to leave Home

As our freshmen year progressed, the relationship between Dad and Andy deteriorated. It seemed as if the only times we saw Dad were when something was going wrong, or at least not to his satisfaction. We were supplying the family with milk, beef, chicken, pork, butter and eggs in addition to firewood for heat, yet there appeared to be little recognition of our efforts. Maybe because Andy was older, Dad held him more responsible, and subjected him to what today would be recognized as mental abuse. Although nobody worked harder than Andy, Dad could only see things to complain about. Late in the fall, the supply pipe carrying drinking water from the spring on the hill across the valley started leaking. On the next Saturday, Dad left Andy alone to do the hard pick and shovel work of digging up the line while he and I went to Cortland for the necessary repair hardware. There was no need to take me to Cortland instead of leaving me to help Andy, but I didn't openly question Dad's orders at the time. It was a miserable cold day, half rain, half snow.

When we came back from Cortland, Andy was gone. Tracks in the melting snow showed a trail up the hill to the south. Mother had not seen him since breakfast, which raised the suspicion that he had run away. Dad's attitude was, "He'll be home when he gets hungry." We finished the digging Andy had started and made the repairs. I went into the woods to the east and found his trail in the melting snow, then lost it, and returned home. It was getting dark, so I started evening chores. Andy, soaked, and really cold, came in the barn. We knew nothing about hypothermia at the time, but he must have been near danger without knowing it. I reported his presence to Mother, and I heard her tell Dad, quite emphatically for her, "He is your son. You better go talk to him!" As Dad went to the barn, I made myself scarce.

I don't know what was said, but after New Year's, a job for room, board, and a small allowance were arranged for Andy on a big dairy farm in the South Otselic School District. The farmer's wife was Dad's cousin. We picked Andy up for church each Sunday morning after chores, so he ate Sunday dinner with the family. The farm family where Andy worked supported him in the extracurricular activities of running track, wrestling, and acting in a play. In spite of the long hard hours of work, he had much more social interaction than Dad would have allowed if he had stayed home.

Managing the Farm

With Andy gone, I assumed full responsibility for the work and management of the farm at the expense of my school work. Morning and evening chores took a lot of time. I only did as much of the assigned school homework as I could during school hours. I kept a passing average by scoring well on tests and the New York State Regents exams. My concerned math teacher sent a note home to my parents to be sure they understood that I was not doing all my homework. Mother signed the note, but the teacher might as well have saved her time.

I started implementing big plans for the future. I planned to increase my herd. To do this, I would need to finish a lean-to expansion structure that Andy and I had started to build on the back side of the barn. I also would need grain, so I planned to convert part of the pasture on the hill across the valley into an oat crop. As the snow thawed in early spring, I blasted out some trees that were in the pasture area I was going to use. I plowed the land and prepared it for seed, but I did not have a grain drill for planting, so I walked over the land sowing the seed broadcast fashion, just as people in the time of Jesus would have done. I had had good results using this method in previous years. The day after I finished planting, a terrible spring rainstorm washed over the whole area. I did not realize that much of my seed had washed down the steep hillside.

Later that spring, Art Leach, an older neighbor with whom I often traded labor, helped me complete the shell of the lean-to. He had always been like a grandfather to me. During the summer, I traded labor with another neighbor to get his and my own hay harvested. I had the tractor with a mower, while he had the baler.

My most embarrassing time

Over the summer, I would often look across the valley at my oat crop which took on an expected nice green shade; so all looked well from a distance. Nobody bothered to take the time to go over there for closer inspection. Later, as the area took on the expected golden brown, Dad said it was time to get someone to harvest it for us. He arranged for Leo Newton, a farmer three miles north of town, to bring a combine and cut the grain. When Leo came, I climbed onto the bagger area of the combine, and we went across the valley and up the hill. To our surprise, the stalks of oats seemed a good six inches apart, or thinner. "I'm sorry to bring you all the way here for this." I apologized. Leo calmly said, "I'm here; let's see what we can get." Around and around the field we went, getting the last oat kernel available. When we finished, we had filled five 100 pound bags. That wasn't 20% of what a normal crop would have been.

After coming back to the house, I again apologized. Sensing my keen embarrassment, Leo said, "I need someone to ride the combine this season; would you like the job?" There was not a sense of derision in his voice or manner! I knew that he had a family of boys, and I doubted that he really needed me. I begged off, saying that I was only fourteen and could not work on school days. I also said that I had too much work to do, such as getting out the winter wood, so I would not be able to accept his offer. Since that day, he has always been one of my secret heroes!

What happened to the cows?—The end of farming

Because I had a real shortage of grain, I had to make adjustments to my plans for the winter of 1956. I saved grain by not raising any more pigs and killing off the remaining chickens. I also butchered the older steer. As the heavy snows started, I had eight cows and first-time heifers bred to calve and produce milk in the late spring. I also had some younger stock for future beef and milk expansion. I started watching the ads for sales of a used milking machine system that I could install over the winter.

I came home from school one day in early spring, went in the house to change my clothes, and then out to do chores. The only cow there was a crippled old Jersey. I looked around for some indication of where the other cattle might be. The fences were not broken; still I found no more animals. I assumed Mother had been home all day, so I went to the house to ask her if she knew anything.

"I wanted your Dad to tell you," She said. "He sold the cows to buy a newer car. You'll have to talk with him about it when he gets home."

When Dad came home, I confronted him about the situation.

"I needed the money to buy a different car," he said.

"What am I supposed to do?" I asked in bewilderment.

Dad explained, "I have talked with Bob Ackley, and he has agreed to take you on as a carpenter's apprentice. You are to start this Saturday. He will pay you $1.00 per hour. I will drive you to De Ruyter; you can ride to wherever the job is with Bob, and I will pick you up at the end of the day."

"What about the money I have spent for breeding fees and grain?" I asked.

Dad reminded me one more time that he owned me and everything I owned. It was a done deal, and I had no say as far as he was concerned.

Looking back, it was again the "Unseen Hand" directing my life. But, at the time, I had no more understanding of what was happening then Biblical Joseph had when his brothers sold him into slavery. On the other hand, carpentry wasn't slavery, and I liked that kind of work. The dollar for every hour worked (minimum wage at the time), was more than I was realizing from the farm. Bob Ackley was my Sunday school teacher, and I was aware that he was a building contractor. The following Saturday morning, I reported to his home at 7:00 a.m. with a hammer, saw, lunch box, and some nervous apprehension about what would be expected of me.

My Apprenticeship Begins

My first job as an apprentice was in Rome, NY, an hour's drive away. I was to cut and fit base boards around the walls of Sunday school rooms in a church that Ackley and Brentlinger Construction Company was remodeling. After about fifteen minutes of orientation and instruction, Bob set me at the task and announced that he would be back to pick me up at five o'clock in the afternoon. He introduced me to Norm, an older carpenter on the job, who was assigned to some other task. If I had questions, I was to ask Norm. I don't know what Dad had told Bob about my skills, but I thought Bob was putting a lot of confidence in an untried new employee. I was determined not to mess up!

At quitting time, Bob showed up and seemed pleased with my work and what I had accomplished. On the ride home he explained their "Christian Builders" philosophy. He said that their accountant, a son-in-law of Emmitt Brentlinger, his partner, would need a set of working papers for the file. I was to get these through the school. I returned to De Ruyter at about 6:00 p.m. and was picked up by Dad. When I got home, I had to go care for that one Jersey cow, but I was much more confident that I could survive and possibly even enjoy this new life.

I worked at one job location or another most Saturdays the rest of the school year. The working papers I obtained clearly stated that workers under sixteen-years-of-age were prohibited from operating power machinery or working on jobs involving the repair, erection, or demolition of buildings. Since I might be doing any of those things on any given day, Bob told me to keep a sharp eye on the driveways. If any vehicle that even looked like it might contain a State Labor Inspector was to pull in, I was to run and hide until the car left. It only happened twice before I became of age. I know how an undocumented worker of today must feel as he works with one eye looking over his shoulder.

Lee R. Clendenning, PhD

Summer, 1956—Serious Construction Training

When school let out in June, I started working full time on the construction of a Baptist Church near Ithaca, NY. We were a non-union crew, which meant that we were not limited to any one construction trade. As carpenters, we set up wooden concrete forms for the foundation and front entrance steps. As concrete workers, we poured and finished the concrete. As masons, we laid block and the finished stone work. As a neophyte, I started in the more common, laborious parts of these tasks which involved moving dirt with a shovel, unloading lumber, block, and stone from delivery trucks, setting up scaffolding, and mixing mortar. There were no fork lift trucks for bulk handling materials then. I hadn't entered into my teen growth spurt, but I was strong and proud that I could hold my own with any man there. I liked participating in all aspects of construction. I learned a lot; and as the work progressed, I was allowed to try my hand at everything. Union crews had specific, vigorously enforced rules about who could do what. The learning opportunities far outweighed the disadvantage of the lower non-union pay scale. Dad decided that I should start paying room and board, so $15.00 of my $32.00 take home pay after taxes went directly to him.

Practical Business Schooling

On our long rides to and from the job, Bob gave me an education regarding the business aspects of building contracting. As the miles were covered, he lectured freely and answered my questions. It was the only business course I ever experienced. We often stopped in route to pick up supplies or coordinate material delivery schedules with suppliers. Coupled with the wide exposure to the various trades, these experiences were later invaluable to me when I did my own small-scale contracting during college days, and when I taught trade related subjects at Virginia Polytechnic Institute, Blacksburg, Virginia, and also at Berry College. Again, the Lord knew what I was going to need, long before I did.

Bob also explained the economics of what he called and practiced as "Christian Contracting." Many of the small congregations we worked for had very limited financial resources, but they usually did have members with some skills willing to volunteer their time for the church. Therefore, Ackley and Brentlinger often arranged a "cost-plus" contract. The church paid for documented costs of material and company labor plus a fixed percentage for overhead expenses. That way any volunteered work would automatically reduce the total cost of the project without anyone having to figure or calculate the value of teens picking up trash, housewives painting woodwork, or farmers nailing down roof shingles. Anything done by volunteers was something we didn't have to do. The system required trust in the cost accounting of the contractor, trust that the work would progress normally without "Gold Bricking" (working slowly to stretch out the job since people were paid by the hour), and also trust that workers would not steal materials or move materials from one job to another. The system also removed the normal risks of loss to the contractor for bad weather or poor estimations. The Company had built up a good reputation among churches in the central New York region. Using the system, a number of small sanctuaries had been built only costing the congregations in the $20,000 to $30,000 range. Mentally, I bought into the system and worked within it as a service to my God.

Chapter 8

1956-1957, Junior Year— Life Changing Accident

When school started in the fall of 1956, I returned to my pattern of Saturday employment. One of Bob's building material suppliers kept him informed when items being sold needed an installer. Bob shifted the tasks to me, so I spent quite a few Saturdays installing such seasonal needs as storm windows, building insulation, and weather stripping. I was looking forward to getting my license to be able to drive myself to and from jobs. I passed the driver's test and received the license in October, but did not have enough money to pay the exorbitant insurance needed for underage male drivers.

The routine fall farm work had to be done in late afternoons after school. The task of getting the winter wood buzz pile ready for the work bee was made easier now because both Art Leach and Uncle Lloyd Foster had gotten chain saws which I borrowed regularly. And, of course, I milked the old Jersey cow. We had plenty of hay for her because during the past summer, Dad had arranged for a local farmer to cut and store the hay crop in exchange for the farmer keeping half of the crop. This arrangement was called "Haying it for the Halves."

Our church needed a good pulpit, so I used my study halls and noon breaks to go to the school shop and make the pulpit. I used cherry lumber from the tree that Andy and I had cut earlier. The new Ag teacher became a good friend who did not object to my presence. The pulpit was delivered to the store-front church just in time for the Fall Evangelistic meetings.

The Life-Changing Accident

For some time, I had been discussing religious questions with my friend, Richard Bell. Richard's family had been active in the Methodist Church in Sheds, NY. Recently, the family had moved to a farm in Quaker Basin, about a mile down the valley from my home, so we rode the school bus together every day. I invited Richard to the special services. After the main service, he responded to the invitation and accepted Jesus Christ as his Savior.

Richard wanted more of his family to hear the gospel. Following the De Ruyter meetings, the Evangelist had scheduled meetings in German, New York, a town about 30 miles away. Although we had licenses, neither Richard nor I could drive after dark until we were seventeen. So Richard talked his older sister, Roberta, into taking us to the meeting on a Thursday night. His brother, Ralph, was also going. To Richard's disappointment, when we arrived at the church, both Roberta and Ralph refused to go in. They said they would pick us up later.

After the meeting, we started home with Roberta and Ralph in the big Buick Roadmaster. I sat behind the driver, and Richard was behind the front passenger seat. The night was pitch black, and the road dry, but unfamiliar to any of us. While I was looking forward, suddenly, without a warning that any of us saw, there was a sharp right bend. Following the curve of the bend was a shallow ditch and high bank. The bank was actually the first thing in view as the lights shone across the ditch. I grabbed the back of the front seat, as poor Roberta screamed in panic. We hit the bank almost head on, climbed the bank, and then careened around the curve to a stop. There were no seat belts in the cars in those days. I remember bouncing up and down between the roof and the big rugged arm rest on the left door like a needle in a sewing machine. As we gathered our wits, I was the only one temporarily disabled. I could not use my legs, and I hurt in my head and the left hip area. They laid me down on the side of the road. A passer-by covered me with her big coat while someone went into a nearby farmhouse to telephone for help. There were no cell phones or 911 services in those days.

Nobody answered the phone at the Bell home. I gave them the Clendenning number, and nobody answered there either. By then, I had feeling and some control back into my right leg. I told them if I could get to the phone, I could convince the operator into letting me talk to the De Ruyter operator. I was sure whoever our "Sarah" was on duty that night would get me help. The De Ruyter operator was Nellie Merchant, a long-time family friend and neighbor. After telling her our trouble and where we were, she said, "Don't worry Lee. Sit tight and I will get someone to help you folks." Knowing everybody, she was able to contact my brother-in law, Keith Hathaway, to come for us. Keith took us directly to Dr. Hamlin's office to be checked. The Doctor was in a foul mood for being awakened in the middle of the night for "nothing but scratches and bruises." By then, I could painfully hobble on my own, so we went home to bed.

The next day, getting out of bed to milk the Jersey was too painful. Dad had to do it. That afternoon, Mother called Patricia and picked her up for a visit. Mother took her home after dark later that evening. I don't think anyone paid Dad his fifteen cents for the call or gas money for the thirty-mile round trip.

When I still couldn't navigate without great pain on Monday following the accident, Mother called Dr. Hamlin. He arranged for an x-ray to be taken at Cortland Memorial Hospital. The x-ray clearly showed a fracture down the left fan of the tailbone, but did not show the much more serious damage to my spine in the lumbar section. I had to wait years until CAT-scan technology was perfected before this damage was clearly described. Dr. Hamlin prescribed rest and limited activity until this fracture healed. I missed school all that week.

I Am Forced Out of the Nest

Dad did not accept my being home in relative idleness gracefully. For the first time in years, I had no income and was not able to pull my own weight. He appeared to view me as a lazy free-loader rather than a son who temporarily needed his care and support. Even as my ability to descend and climb the cellar stairs to tend the furnace, bring in wood from the woodshed, and sit on the stool and milk the cow returned, I became the target of his abuse. As we went into the holiday season, it clearly was time for me to get out of the nest. But, where could I go? I still was not physically ready to work for room and board on a farm. I could quit school, but I wasn't physically able to return to construction. I really didn't ask the Lord, "Why me?" because I honestly believed that I would have a short term recovery and pick up where I had left off.

Without my knowledge, as He would do so many times in the future, the Unseen Hand was working on a solution to my problems. Suddenly, in the middle of an academic year, a part-time janitorial assistance position opened at the school. I was asked by the Business Manager if I wanted the job. Of course, I did! The job hours would be from school dismissal until 9:00 pm on school days with time out for supper. The job would start after Christmas break, and I would need to rent a room in town through the week.

Mable Crump to the Rescue

Mother and I went to town looking for a room to rent. My relatives in town turned me down, as did a local bread and breakfast. Then, somehow, Mable Crump came to mind. My sisters were no longer working in her nursing facility, but we knew she had a big house. An older divorcee, Mable was a little bitter over life's trials, and she always spoke quite frankly and sharp. When we arrived she said, "I wondered when you would get here. You have been all over town, and I am your last hope!" Word travels fast in a small town! She was right, of course. She continued, "You can eat breakfast and supper here. I will need five dollars per week; and if you expect me to do your laundry, I will need fifty cents more."

I could have kissed her! That was one third what my own father would have charged me! Mable showed us a small room with a bed, a study table, and an adjacent bath. She lived on South Hill, across town about three-quarters of a mile from the school. I had walked that far on the farm most days of my life.

As I came and went, sharing meals and conversation with Mable, she became a good friend. With age, her business had declined to only one bedridden patient and the care of a young boy, Bobby, who had what appeared to be Down's syndrome. On the first evening, after the three of us sat down for supper, I quietly bowed my head and said a short grace, just between me and the Lord. We enjoyed a good meal, making small talk about my new job. When I returned for bed-time, there were a piece of pie, a glass of milk, and a note for me to enjoy them on the kitchen table. The next morning as we started breakfast, I again bowed my head. I heard an authoritative voice, "If you are going to do that every meal, you might as well say grace for all of us!" I did then and every meal after that. As I came into the kitchen for a meal, Mable would have Bobby already in his high chair. Bobby would say, repeatedly, "Can't eat till Lee says grace; can't eat till Lee says grace." Mable had known my Grandmother Clendenning, so she was able to fill me in on some details of my grandmother's life.

Good school guidance

In my junior year, Mr. David Fish was the guidance teacher. In the fall, before the accident, he scheduled me for a conference. In spite of my disinterest in his professional help, he persisted in doing his job (Thank the Lord!). Mr. Fish recommended an engineering career and gave me literature from what I now know to be first-rate engineering schools. I had no concept of engineering beyond Uncle Lloyd Foster's operating a train on the New York Central. I kept assuring Mr. Fish that I had no interest in college. He backed off for a while.

After the tail-bone healed, my physical discomfort refocused on the lumbar section of my spine. I did not consider sweeping rooms, emptying paper baskets, and washing blackboards to be heavy work compared to construction, but this kind of work still hurt. One day I went into the Guidance Office and asked Mr. Fish if there were any other college programs that might be of interest. He asked me if I thought I would like to be an industrial arts teacher.

"Industrial Arts, what is that?" I asked.

He explained that it was an educational program in larger schools in which students were taught how to make projects using tool skills in woodworking, metalworking, and mechanical drawing. Now that did sound interesting. He arranged a field trip for the two of us to go to Oswego State Teachers College and "look around."

On the eighty-mile trip to Oswego, NY, Mr. Fish talked more about industrial arts and vocational-industrial shop teaching in general. I learned that the educational bureaucrats in Washington, DC, would only fund Vocational-Industrial Education in city areas, and Agriculture Education in rural areas. That was why we only had a farm shop in our school. Industrial Arts was an elective part of general education charged with the development of manual skills and understandings that would be useful regardless of which trade, profession, or leisure time hobby a person chose. The subject was not necessarily supported everywhere. Oswego State had the largest Industrial Arts teacher preparation program in the world, and I had never heard of it.

As we toured the teacher preparation shops, I never dreamed that heaven was so close. There were multiple lathes, planers, drill presses, table saws, milling machines, and machines I did not recognize, all neatly organized in spaced rows so that they could be used by many students simultaneously. The tool racks on the walls stored every hand tool I had ever seen. In addition to woodworking and metalworking, there were separate shops for auto mechanics, transportation, textiles, ceramics/pottery, graphic arts/printing, electricity/electronics, and drafting/design. Students were required to take a basic course in all these areas and then specialize in at least two with advanced courses. They would then graduate with New York State certification to teach the basics of all of them. I was sold! I didn't know how, and I didn't know when, but I determined that somehow, someday, I was going to Oswego!

The field trip with Mr. Fish was another life changing experience. With a definite goal in mind, I took much more interest in getting my homework completed and submitted on time. I started planning to cut a big maple tree to have material ready for projects in the future. I envisioned that the life of an industrial arts teacher would be much less physically demanding and fully as interesting as my previous experiences in construction. The dream, however, seemed like a pie in the sky for someday in the future. In the meantime, I still had to earn my living as a student janitor.

During this same spring, Richard Bell started a Bible study with some of his friends meeting once a week after school in an empty classroom. I could only encourage from a distance because of my work. This small group also started regularly attending our Sunday evening Youth Fellowship. Richard was a positive influence on more of our peers in six months than I had been able to reach in my life-time. After graduation, he studied for the ministry.

The school job also limited my contact with Patricia to Saturday evenings and church-related meetings on Sunday. At the end of the spring semester, she graduated from Fabius Central School and enrolled in Powelson Business Institute, Syracuse, NY, with a scholarship. She majored in accounting, but she also had to study office practices, business law, business English, and office machines. She worked part-time during her schooling.

Summer, 1957,—Work, pain, and confirmation

On the last Friday of the school year, the Business Manager asked me if I wanted to stay on for full time work for the summer. At first it sounded like a good idea, so I said I would. But then she went on to say, "Lee, you are doing so good; when you graduate next year, you can stay on permanently. Doc Messenger will be retiring; you can take his place." Thinking about the conversation on the way home, I was troubled. I didn't want to be trapped in a school janitor's job for the rest of my life. I told the folks about the offer over supper. Dad was negative. "Do you want to be known as a janitor or a carpenter [his goal for me]? You are developing your reputation now." Then I panicked. As irrational as it sounds now, at the time, I was not going to be trapped if I could help it.

I called Bob Ackley and explained that I had recovered to the point that I could work construction if he would let me perform the work at my own pace and in my own way. I asked if I could have a job for the summer. He agreed to hire me again on my terms. He was building a small church sanctuary in a community just east of Syracuse. The following Monday morning, I entered the Business Manager's Office, thanked her for the job offer, and said I would be going back to work for Bob. She was stunned, but I did not explain the real reason for my leaving. She asked about the next fall. I burned my bridge behind me and said that I would not be working for the school then either.

I needed transportation in a hurry so I used money I had squirreled away to fix up the old 1948 Chevy Dad had set aside when he sold the cows. I had enough to buy the parts and to add an underage male driver to Dad's insurance policy. To my relief, he never asked me where I got the funds. I arranged for room and board with Aunt Elsena and Uncle Louis Hanes in East Syracuse. I still could not drive after dark, but I felt a new burst of freedom.

The work was tough enough that I was forced to seek further medical help. We were in the concrete and building block phase as I started. One of the volunteers who worked every Wednesday after mid-week service sensed my plight and recommended a chiropractor in the area. One evening, I went there, and the doctor crunched me around some. I made an appointment for an additional treatment the following week. When those were obviously not effective, the chiropractor was honest enough to admit he could not help me. He sent me to an osteopathic physician who took an x-ray of my lumbar spine. He explained that the x-ray only showed the bony parts of the spine and provided little information about the disks and internal spinal cord. He couldn't see anything wrong with the disks, but he did prescribe a corset-like back brace for me to try. The brace did help tremendously. This was long before such braces were commonly seen on lumber yard warehouse workers. When I returned to him, he told me to find some other line of work. "You are young enough to go to college and make your living with your brain instead of your brawn!" he emphasized.

"But won't I eventually heal with time?"

He answered that I had given the tail bone plenty of time to heal, but in his experience, internal damage to the spinal cord was a life-time condition. "Go to college!" he again advised.

Lee R. Clendenning, PhD

A Short Lawsuit

When I went home wearing the white corset, I finally got the family's attention that I might have a real problem. Mother and Dad agreed that we should seek the advice of a lawyer. In researching the case, the lawyer got a statement from Dr. Hamlin that my fracture had healed, and I should only be awarded my immediate medical expenses. The lawyer learned that there was no police report of the accident, that I had gone to work for the school within sixty days of the accident, and that I was currently working construction. Given these facts, he didn't have much hope for a big settlement. The first offer he obtained from the insurance company was $900. He advised us to settle for that, and we did. Given today's climate of pain and suffering awards, $900 sounds like the pittance that it was. Since I was a minor, the $600 left after the lawyer's fee was deposited in a bank in care of my Dad. Later that fall, Dad and I withdrew some of it to purchase a used radial arm saw. Much later, I purchased Patricia's engagement and wedding rings with what was left. Patricia is still wearing the rings, so I did receive some tangible benefit from the accident beyond changing my career and confirmation that I should go to college.

How to pop a prideful balloon

In spite of my discomfort, I continued work on the East Syracuse church building. When we got the roof trusses placed, Bob assigned me to build the small steeple. Rather than purchasing a ready-made steeple and hoisting it onto the roof with a crane as is the practice in today's construction world, we had to integrate the supporting structure into the roof framing. Then the exterior of the steeple was sided and shingled one piece at a time. It was a challenge, but I could work alone at my own pace. I was really proud of the finished product.

After church on a Sunday afternoon, I took Patricia for a drive stopping in front of the church. We got out of the car, stood on the sidewalk to the entrance, and looked up at the new building.

"How do you like the steeple?" I asked innocently.

She cocked her head to one side, squinted one eye, and shifted her weight from one foot to another while clouds hung in waiting against a blue sky.

Finally, she said, "It's crooked."

To this day, she swears she was deliberately trying to be funny. But, I was not amused. We drove by the church about fifty years later. I was pleased to see that in spite of various additions to the church facilities, my steeple was still standing as I had built it.

Beginning Self-employment

As the summer was coming to an end, I had to lay plans for the fall. I didn't want to go back to the school and beg for my janitorial job. Since Dad seemed pleased that I had chosen construction for the summer, and since all of my sisters were no longer home, I proposed to move my bedroom upstairs in the house and convert the back lean-to room into a custom woodworking shop for self-employment. I hoped to earn enough to pay for my room and board at home and keep the car on the road. Dad liked the idea. He thought I should forget about "college nonsense" and establish myself as a self-employed tradesman. I didn't want to fight the college war with him then, but I took advantage of his moral support for the creation of a shop. By then, I had acquired the jointer, router, table saw, radial arm saw, power sander, and small thickness planer. My shop was complete, and I used it intermittently from then until I graduated from college.

Dad's attitude toward me mellowed as he faced the possible reality of cutting his own firewood. He was also starting to develop shortness of breath and tired feelings, symptoms of his then undiagnosed heart disease. He bought a chain saw and sold the old Jersey. Later in the fall, he even helped me cut one of the giant maple trees and take the logs to a saw mill so that I would have quality material to work with. I still have a couple of boards from that tree. That was the day a flying limb broke off my lower front tooth. I was still spitting blood on my date with Patricia that night, so, no goodnight kiss.

Chapter 9

God Provides a Scholarship

Early in my senior year, Mr. Fish took a small busload of college prep students to Morrisville Ag and Tech School to take our college entrance exam. On the way over, he told us that we should skip questions when we did not immediately know the answer, and then come back to them if time allowed at the end. It was the first time I had seen a "fill in the bubble" answer sheet. Upon going back through the test items, I discovered that when I skipped a question I did not always skip the corresponding bubble on the answer sheet. Through erasures, I tried to correct my sheet, but I knew some responses were still in the wrong place as the papers were collected. In the blanks at the test heading, I listed Oswego State as the place to send the results even though I had not yet applied to go there.

Then, late in one lunch period while I was killing time with the Ag teacher, a voice from heaven said, "Is Lee Clendenning out in the shop?" It was the public address intercom system.

The teacher hollered back, "Yes."

"Then send him to the cafeteria immediately!" the voice said.

"OK," the teacher responded.

As I entered the cafeteria, Mr. Fish greeted me with, "Hurry! You are already behind! You sit right over there." As I took my seat, I glanced around and saw all the college prep students of my class working like beavers on what looked like a test with the bubble answering sheet. These were students who did all of their homework, every day. Looking at my booklet on the desk in front of me, I read, "**New York State Regents College Scholarship Test.**" I thought, "Why didn't I know about this?" I knew the answer. I was too busy making a living to pay close attention to what was going on in school.

After my college entrance test experience, I took extra care to get all test answers marked beside correct numbers on the score sheet. There was an essay section asking us to select a famous person from a short list and describe the significance of his or her contributions to humanity. I selected Dr. Jonas Salk. I identified his contribution as the development of the polio vaccine, the only fact I really knew about him. I repeated my Dad's often related tale of being a young boy looking out of a window watching other children run and play while wishing he could join them. I made sure the reader/grader would know that the boy was my father recovering from polio. (When you don't have the facts, look for sympathy.) Because of Dr. Jonas Salk, millions of potential victims of the disease would not suffer that way. Again, I listed Oswego State as my potential college and submitted my papers. The next week, following Mr. Fish's advice, I formally applied for admission to Oswego State.

I had forgotten about the scholarship test when one morning teachers passing me in the hall hesitated long enough to say, "Congratulations, Lee." The same words came from a couple of my peers in the home room.

When I asked, "For what?" Someone said, "Didn't you read the Cortland paper this morning? [We didn't subscribe to a daily paper.] You were the only person listed from De Ruyter to get a Regents Scholarship!" I was stunned.

About then, the public address system again asked, "Is Lee Clendenning there?"

I recognized the Principal's voice and replied "Yes, I am here."

"Come to the office," he commanded.

The Principal was short and to the point when I arrived. "Don't get excited about what is in the paper this morning," he said. "There has been a foul-up in Albany. I will call them later this morning and straighten things out."

Talk about a yo-yo of emotions. I said, "OK," and left for my first class.

For the rest of the day I simply said, "Thank you," anytime someone congratulated me as I waited for further word from the Principal. I will never know whether he really called Albany. All I do know is that he never called me back in to discuss the situation, and I didn't go to him looking for bad news. I also know that if the Lord hadn't sent someone to summon me to the test, there would have been no scholarship for me.

My letter of announcement from the State briefly described the details of the scholarship. The scholarships were renewable for four years as long as one maintained a continuous enrollment and a passing grade average. The school listed on the test form would be notified directly of the award. That seemed fair enough to me. I finally got an acceptance letter from Oswego assigning me a dorm room and a date to appear.

Finally, a serious student

With a college career clearly possible in a course of study that excited me, for the first time, my studies became the most important aspect of my life. I missed no more school days the rest of the year, only working enough to support my car and the single date her mother would allow with Patricia each week. I did my homework. I finished the year with the highest senior average, earning the Senior Cup at graduation. I was one of four Salutatorians with averages that the school called too close to separate us. The honors of Valedictorian and Salutatorian were based on our accumulated four-year averages. I wrote the class poem which was read at our Class Night celebration. On graduation afternoon, I had to make a short address. The Principal publically announced my scholarship. I had encouraged the rest of my family to attend Andy's graduation in South Otselic on that same day, but Patricia was there to congratulate me. I felt like the Lord was in control, and I would be fulfilling His plan for me.

Misunderstanding scholarship administration and disappointment

As I worked for Bob during the summer, I kept looking for more communication about my scholarship. I only received another letter from Oswego showing how much I owed and confirming the deadline for payment and the date for my arrival. At first I didn't worry about the payment because I believed they knew about my scholarship. Patricia requested time off from her work to take me to Oswego on the specified date. The morning before we were to leave, I grew nervous over the finances and suddenly felt that something was wrong. I called the Oswego Admissions Office to see if they had my scholarship funds. The answer was, No! Scholarship funds would not be credited to my account until I had completed my first semester with posted passing grades.

I was shocked. "You mean I have to finance my first semester myself?"

"Of course," was the short answer. You will get one-half of your yearly stipend at the end of each semester as long as you keep your grades up," the voice continued.

"But, I don't have the money; I was counting on the scholarship," I complained.

"If the fees are not paid by tomorrow's deadline, we will have no choice but to cancel your enrollment," the voice responded.

At that time, there were no Pell grants, not even an Office of Financial Aid. If a student didn't have the funds on time, he or she didn't go.

"Don't cancel me yet," I pleaded. "I'll see what I can do and call you back."

After ending this first call, I apprised Mother of the new understandings. I promised to turn the scholarship check over to Dad and her in January if they would borrow what I needed. I knew that they had no debt and good credit. She called Dad at his work. He said absolutely not; he didn't want me to go to college anyway. Besides, if the fall charges were paid back from the January check, he would have to borrow again for the spring charges.

I called Oswego back and asked whether I would lose the scholarship completely if I did not use it this semester. The lady was more sympathetic this time. She explained that in "hardship cases" a one-time leave of absence from the scholarship for a year could be granted. The deadline for such a request for the current academic year was that day! Since I was a minor, a parent or guardian would have to sign the form validating the request. I told her that my mother and I would be there as soon as possible to submit our request. Mother and I left immediately for Oswego. We submitted the proper forms to postpone my admission for a year, cancel my housing assignment, and hold my scholarship. On our way home from Oswego, Mother and I stopped in Fabius to tell Patricia the new developments. She was as shocked as I had been and disappointed that I had had no opportunity to discuss my actions with her before they were a done deal. My failure to go to college at that point added fuel to her mother's repeated rant, "He will never amount to anything anyway."

Although my inability to finance my entrance into college as planned was a big disappointment at the time, in retrospect, this was part of the Master's plan. Little did any of us know that in twelve years I would need specialized certification as a vocational-industrial teacher trainer. A minimum of 2,000 hours of documented employment in a trade at the journeyman level was required by the Federal Vocational Education Act of 1963 in order to accept a faculty position at Virginia Polytechnic Institute, and later, the position at Berry College. By working for Ackley and Brentlinger full time that year instead of going to college, I acquired the hours I needed. Potential industrial arts teachers did not have an occupational requirement. By both of us working during that year, Patricia and I were able to save enough money to start our marriage and cover the charges for my first semester the following year. Again, the Lord knew what He was doing even if I felt like I was floundering.

Chapter 10

Sharing Married and College Life Together

Patricia and I were married on June 6, 1959, in an outdoor wedding on the Terrill's side lawn. Patricia's Grandfather Adsitt had cut and placed small evergreen trees to form a backdrop for an altar area. Flowers were used to further define the location of the ceremonial vows. Borrowed folding chairs were arranged with an isle in the center to accommodate around 150 guests. A local lady was recruited to play the small Thomas organ which we had acquired as our mutual gift to each other. Beverly Farewell, one of Patricia's high school friends, was the Maid of Honor. Darlene Mulvena, a daughter of long-time friends of the family, was the Bride's Maid, and Patricia's sister, Evelyn, was a Junior Bride's Maid. Andy was my Best Man, and the ushers were Richard Bell and Patricia's brother, Douglas. Patricia was beautiful in her ballroom-length white dress. It was, and still is, the happiest day of my life.

During an afternoon reception with nuts, mints, punch, and cake made by Patricia's mother, we opened our gifts. I was shocked at the number and variety of practical things we received because I had been given very little in life up to that point. Our guests really set us up for housekeeping. We are still using a few of the kitchen items!

We left for a short honeymoon in the Adirondack Mountains, since Patricia wanted to return by the following Wednesday evening to keep the Guest Register at the fiftieth wedding anniversary celebration of Bernard and Grace Rowley. Grace was her great aunt on her mother's side. I also needed time to set up our mobile home. We "camped out" in that eight by thirty-five foot unit for the next four years.

We continued to work at our respective jobs in the Syracuse area until it was nearly time to report to Oswego. A "divine appointment" supplied the job we needed for Patricia in the college area. One day, I was discussing our plans and needs with the Pastor of the church we were remodeling. He told me to tell Patricia to go to the Dilts Division of the Black Clawson Co. in Fulton, NY, and ask for Frank. The office was only 15 miles from where our trailer would be parked. She was to use the Pastor she had never met as a reference. Patricia did as instructed and was promised a job with health benefits for both of us and as much overtime as she wanted to work. I quit my job and supervised the movement of the trailer, setting it up again in a park near the campus.

From then on, we settled into a routine for work, school, and housekeeping. Whether our families understood it or not, working as a team without regard to the old farm-based expectations for gender was the only way we could survive. Failure was not an option. Patricia commuted with the car, dropping me off at the college early in the morning, and I arranged rides home with fellow students in the late afternoon. We both carried our lunches, but I could have a hot supper all ready for her by the time she got home in the evening. After supper, I would wash the dishes as she typed my homework papers to be submitted, usually the next day. I also took care of the laundry on the machines maintained by the park management and did the ironing, as there were no permanent press fabrics back then. Patricia worked late most days each week and usually Saturday mornings. We returned to Fabius on those weekends when I had sold a project needing my shop. I did occasional small repairs, solved electrical problems in Oswego's older homes, remodeled rooms, and built custom bookcases and cupboards for professors.

Beginning college classes

In the early 1960's, Oswego was using the old "washout" method of controlling the size and quality of the student body. Many more students than could reasonably be accommodated in the higher classes were accepted into a new freshman class. In one of the Freshmen Orientation meetings, the Dean said, "Look at the individuals on each side of you. By November, one of them will be missing. By the start of the spring semester, there is a good chance that the other one will be gone." I determined that I was the one staying!

Classes were pre-scheduled by major, leaving no personal choices. One studied the prescribed courses at the times and in the sequence that curriculum designers preplanned. Looking back with some perspective now, I realize I had excellent professors that first semester. I was assigned Drafting/Design, Basic Mathematics, Beginning Woodworking, Introduction to Psychology, and Introduction to Speech. Each professor explained that the majority of us would do average work, so two-thirds of us would receive C's. B's were only awarded for "Above Average" work, and the rare A's were for "Excellent" work beyond what was assigned. There would be only mid-term and final tests. We were to be evaluated on "Attitude" as well as projects and tests, and poor attendance was considered reflective of a bad attitude.

I soon learned that I had little in common with the students my own age. I felt like a crude country bumpkin to those with city backgrounds. In each class, there were a number of older, married, military veterans taking advantage of the G.I. Bill. They became my friends and academic peers in spite of the age differences. At lunch time, we would discuss the assignments, the professor's requirements, and our possible responses. They were a great support group who respected my opinions as they freely shared their own.

I survived my first clash of culture with my psychology professor. He was a young fellow who apparently felt it necessary to impress the veterans with his ability to curse, which he did with regularity. I finally raised my hand. When he called on me, I knew he was expecting a question about the subject at hand, but I said, "Do you have to swear so often?"

He was blind-sided, but he recovered. "Why do you ask? Does it offend you?"

One of my new veteran friends was slinking down in his desk beside mine, trying to pretend he didn't know me.

I simply said, "Yes."

By then the professor was defensive. "I'll have you know that in middle class society, when one wants to emphasize a point, they use profanity."

Without thinking how I was going to sound as the class hick who used the word "ain't" and wrong tenses of verbs way too often, I said, "It seems to me like a mark of ignorance if you can't express yourself without it."

Now he was really blind-sided! After a long pause, he said, "Let's get back to the topic of the day."

That evening we happened to be with the slinking veteran. He told Patricia that I had just flunked the psychology course. But often in class sessions after that, when the professor would start to curse, he would look at me, choose some other word and continue. At the end of the course, I was pleased to see my A grade in psychology.

I also made the mistake of complaining to the Department Chair about the simplicity of the Basic Mathematics course. I had mastered everything in the course text by ninth grade, and I wanted to study calculus. He was indignant that I had brass enough to question the curriculum.

"Shop boys don't need calculus!" he said. "I've had other boys think they were so smart. They went into the Math Department, flunked the course, and made us look bad. You will be lucky if you don't flunk out of here by Thanksgiving. If you can get a good, easy grade in math, you are going to need the quality points to maintain a passing grade point average."

I gave up and started spending time tutoring the veterans who had not studied math in years.

The truth of the Dean's orientation speech was supported on the day of the scheduled mid-term tests. Pointing to some empty desks, I asked nobody in particular, "Where is everybody?"

Someone responded, "They went home yesterday. They were too chicken to face the tests."

I was surprised! "I'm not going to flunk out without even trying," I said.

Another incident related to my simple background reinforced my conviction that I was following the Master's plan for me. As I was walking down the hall with my mid-term grade report, a young classmate stopped me.

"Let me see your report," he demanded as he snatched it out of my hand. He inspected it. "Why your grades are better than mine!" He exclaimed loudly.

I was speechless. He went into a rage: "You are nothing but a Hillbilly Hick! You have no business even being in college! How did you get better grades than me?"

I was still speechless. How should I respond? Before I could say anything, he returned my grade sheet and was gone. Realizing there was some truth in his description of me I started to feel a little downcast.

Just then God's spirit spoke to me very clearly. "Don't worry about that kid," the Spirit said. "Someday he will call you looking for a job."

Like Mary in the Bible, over the years I "pondered" that message in my heart. It was my confirmation that I had chosen the right career.

Sure enough, years later I sat in my office at Berry College when the phone rang. That same student had become a committed Christian and was looking for a college teaching position. He gave me a short but strong testimony. Since we had not advertised a faculty position, and I did not know of any immediate openings, I could not help him. He said he was puzzled because he thought he had God's leading to call me. He hoped as a fellow Christian I would understand his bothering me. I assured him that it was good to hear from him and about his commitment to Christ. I assured him I would pass any word about new positions along to him. I did not remind him of our earlier confrontation; I knew exactly why he had called. God keeps His promises!

A change in industrial arts specialty

In January, at the end of the fall semester, Patricia and I were pleased to see me listed on the Dean's list. The scholarship funds were assured, but my plans, seemingly on track, were suddenly modified by choices beyond my control. My schedule included Physics I, English Composition, Woodworking II, Intro to Metalworking, Shop

Mathematics II, and Physical Education (Swimming). In the first session of the Woodworking II class, as we waited for instruction to start, the Curriculum Coordinator appeared in front of the group. "The State has plenty of woodworking teachers," he said. "They need more people in this new field called electronics; I have been over your high school records to see who has the necessary math. Clark, Clendenning, Green, ... , you boys go upstairs and study electronics." Nobody dared say a word; we gathered our notebooks and went upstairs. I still had to complete the rest of the teacher preparation program for industrial arts, but from then on, my specialty would be electronics. That ended my dream of being the world's greatest woodworker. I have been involved in electronics throughout the rest of my career. My future options and opportunities were greatly multiplied by this forced action. Again, God knew what He was doing.

My mentor, Mr. Orla Loper

During my first class session in physics, it became clear that the course would be a repeat of my high school experience. After class I asked the professor, Mr. Orla Loper, if there was a college level physics course being offered.

He replied, "Sure, I teach it."

I asked if I could take that course rather than the current one. He quizzed me about my high school physics Regents test.

"I got a 97 because I missed part of a question on atomic energy."

"That is better than most of my science majors."

Mr. Loper checked my printed schedule and concluded that I could fit in both the labs and lectures. Then he added; "Go tell your Department Head that I said it would be OK to swap enrollments in the courses."

The Department Head was not happy to see me again, and he said what I wanted to do was impossible as far as he was concerned. But, he said that I could appeal to the Dean if I wished. I did. The Dean was polite but firm. In his opinion, mixing students from different majors into the hard sciences was not a good practice. In defeat, I reported back to Mr. Loper.

"Just a minute," he said as he wrote on a piece of paper while I waited politely. When finished, he folded the paper and put it in an envelope.

"Take this to the Dean," he commanded.

Obediently, I took the note to the Dean without reading it. The Dean's face turned red as he read the message.

"Ok," he said, "I guess we can approve your request." He, in turn, wrote on the paper and said, "Take this down to the Department Head."

I did as ordered. The Department Head, obviously agitated, read the note and said; "Tell Loper to work out the details."

When I reported to Mr. Loper, he only said, "I'll see you in the lecture Tuesday."

Mr. Loper became a good friend and mentor. I learned that he was the person who manually worked out all the schedules of classes for the entire institution. This was before punched computer card registrations. Days before a semester was to begin, his office desk and work tables would be piled high with stacks of student schedules. When I discussed transfer to an engineering school in order to study calculus, he said; "You don't need to do that." He moved whole piles around so that I could take my calculus sequence with the math majors, chemistry with chemistry majors, physics with those majors, and still meet all my required industrial arts courses. Because of him, I was prepared to minor in mathematics and statistics on the Master's and PhD levels. In the course of time, I remodeled his home, and much later, co-authored a basic electronics book with him. I believe God placed Mr. Loper in my path to make it possible for a "shop boy" to get a real rigorous education.

God had fought an Unseen Battle for Me

I was surprised by a letter from the Admissions Office which stated "Congratulations! You have been removed from probation status." I took the letter into that office and asked, "What is this all about?"

The Director of Admissions explained that I had been admitted to the college on probation. Since I was now on the Dean's list, probation had been lifted.

I asked the natural question, "Why was I on probation?" Her reply humbled me.

"When you applied, we already had your college entrance test scores. Your score was so low in English that you would be automatically rejected," she explained. "But, when the Regents Scholarship letter came, I reopened your application. The Admissions Committee argued about you for three hours one morning. I argued that maybe you just had a bad day on the entrance test. Others said that bad day or not, anyone scoring that low was not college material. Still another said that we would take a lot of political heat if it were made known that we would not admit a holder of a Regents Scholarship. At lunch time, we compromised and agreed to admit you on probation. Your achievement of the Dean's list vindicated that decision."

I could hardly believe it! God had raised a couple of champions willing to fight for three hours to save my career, and I didn't even know there had been a battle! Further, my messing up the bubble markings on my entrance test had been nullified. The voice I had heard calling me to take the Regents Scholarship test took on even more significance. Others can call such events lucky random coincidences, but I saw the Master's plan.

Lansing's Corners Friends Church

Immediately after moving to Oswego, Patricia and I started looking for a place to worship and fellowship on the Sundays we didn't return to Fabius. We visited a couple of places a number of times, but did not settle into a church during the first year. I was finally led to our church home by another "Divine Appointment." As I looked for work at a small lumber yard east of Fulton, I was hired for the remainder of the day to help another tradesman install two, big replacement windows.

My new coworker greeted me on the job and said, "I'll handle the inside work while you do the outside from the ladder."

Revealing the Unseen Hand

That was fine with me. As we were picking up our tools after finishing the job, he said, "My brother needs a good man on his crew. Would you be interested?" Of course I was! He added, "By the way, my brother is a preacher; think you could work with a preacher?"

"I wouldn't let that bother me," I replied.

After giving me his brother's telephone number, as he left, he remarked, "Tell him Chubb sent you."

I called the number that evening, told the voice on the phone that Chubb had told me to call, and asked if he needed help.

"Yes, I do," was his short reply. I learned later that he had difficulty hearing, and therefore, he didn't talk much on the phone. He gave me a job address to report to at eight the following morning.

The job in progress was painting a big, three story brick house. I didn't question why anyone would want to paint over well preserved brick, but I did see why he needed help. There was a lot of ladder and scaffold work. His only help were two brothers who appeared to be in their late teens or early twenties. I was assigned the south wall while the brothers worked together on the west wall. When we met one time at the corner, one of them said, "By the way, watch what you say around the boss; he's a preacher."

"That won't bother me, where does he preach?"

"Out at Lansing's Corners" was the answer. I had no idea where that was.

Curiosity got the best of me when the boss reappeared to eat his lunch with us.

"I understand you are a preacher," I ventured.

"Yes," was his brief reply.

The boys had already told me where, so I didn't want to appear stupid to them by asking that question again. After a few silent mouthfuls, I thought maybe I could find out more.

"Where did you go to school to become a preacher?"

"The school of hard knocks," he replied with a slight smile.

I dropped the quizzing. On the second day at lunch, I asked about the payment process. I learned that the boss' wife was the bookkeeper, business manager, and payroll clerk for Crouch Construction Company.

The boss's name was Jim Crouch. In addition to my name, the boss had to have my social security number, and address for me to get paid.

While Jim was in a talkative mood, I quizzed him some more about his church.

"Where was Lansing's Corners?"

"Three miles out Hall Road."

"How many services do you have each week?"

"Three."

"How large is the congregation?"

"Mostly my family."

"What are your services like?"

"We sing and I preach, but, we don't have anyone to play the piano now."

That was the longest sentence I had gotten out of him. One of the helpers had told me, "Jim doesn't talk much except when he is preaching."

"My wife plays the piano," I informed him.

By the end of the week, in short exchanges, Jim and I had established that we were fellow followers of Christ. He invited Patricia and me to visit his church on Sunday.

Lansing's Corners was a cross-roads community about three miles east of the Oswego city line. A big, old church building sat near one of the four corners. The building had been previously abandoned for a number of years before being taken over by Reverend Jim Crouch's small congregation. The sign out front said, "Lansing Friends Church." It wasn't clear whether the sign was a relic of past history, or something Jim had put there a few years ago. Upon hearing about the sign, Patricia's mother concluded that they were Quakers. We thought they were friendly; but if they were Quakers, I doubt if they knew it.

There may have been twenty people present when we visited that first Sunday Morning. Patricia played the piano for the congregation to sing. One voice from the rear was the most crystal clear soprano I have ever heard. We learned it came from Jim's married daughter. Jim's sermon, like those we heard to follow, was mostly personal testimony centered on a particular scripture reading. Clearly, he knew and loved the Lord in a really personal way. He liked the scriptures in the first three chapters of the Book of Hebrews where Christ is presented as a new and better message from God than the angels (Hebrews 1:4), worthy of more glory than Moses (Hebrews 3:3). He had personally found that "Better One," and shared his faith.

As we became better acquainted with our new church family, we learned their history from Jim's more talkative sisters. The big Crouch clan had been raised in the Lansing area. Many of Jim's generation had a few years of one room schooling and worked as laborers in the "muck land" agriculture of the area. Muck was what they appropriately called the naturally wet, coal black soil in the lake plains. Labor intensive crops like onions and strawberries thrived there. Jim Crouch migrated to the Cleveland, Ohio, area to work in a defense industry during World War II. In Ohio, he married and also discovered the "better way," committing his life to Christ. He and his wife were led to return to the Lansing area to share his faith with his extended clan. He preached, his wife played the piano, and they taught Sunday school in the old church. They were successful in winning many of Jim's brothers and sisters to their faith.

Sometime before Patricia and I arrived, tragedy struck Jim's family. The oldest son drowned in what I understand to be a military accident in Alaska. Jim's wife became bitter against God for allowing this to happen, and withdrew from supporting his ministry. Jim carried on the work of the church alone. When we arrived, the congregation was composed largely of his brothers and sisters and their grandchildren. Except for Jim's married daughter, his younger daughter, and a couple of other nieces and nephews, the intervening generation was largely absent. There was no formal church organization for governance such as trustees, deacons, elders, or connections to a higher denomination's expectations. The congregation was eager for leadership, particularly in teaching the children and providing music during worship.

Patricia and I were soon adopted into the clan. They brought us home-baked goods in appreciation for our efforts and included us in informal social parties in their homes, again with great food. When our food budget for a week was $7.00, every soft roll counted! I think many of today's college age students miss the benefits and personal satisfaction to be found in a simple place of service rather than looking for a church which meets their entertainment needs.

Our presence did seem to inject a new sense of hope in the church. Jim was already teaching an adult Sunday school class, and I soon started a youth class with about six teenagers. Patricia started working with another woman in teaching a growing children's class. Neighborhood children unrelated to Jim's clan started to attend. One of Jim's older brothers told Patricia if she would teach him to sing in a choir, he would buy some new teeth. Patricia and I sang a duet once in a while. We couldn't get the daughter with the perfect voice to sing a solo, but Patricia did initiate a choir of six to nine voices. She directed as she played with a couple of keys in the middle of the old piano not functioning. Today, I am glad there are no recordings of us. We had the right spirit anyway. Patricia did organize a "Singspiration" where our church hosted people and musicians from other small congregations. Our people supplied the supper feast. At Christmas time, I mounted a wire across the front of the church platform so that we could hang a curtain for a Christmas play. We used the wire for two Christmas and Easter programs.

Listen Carefully to Your Wife

One time when he was going to be gone, Jim asked me to lead the Wednesday night service. I decided that I would use Socrates' method of teaching rather than preach or lecture. After all, I was in training to be a teacher. This method involves asking leading questions, bringing the learner or audience to the desired conclusion. I had my questions all organized and ready. It was below zero outside and not much above freezing inside. As I started the service, the small faithful group huddled in the first two pews, still wearing their outside coats. At the piano, Patricia stiff-fingered the opening song as I led. When I presented the first question, there was no response. I repeated it. Still no response, so I answered my own question, leading to the next one. Although they were given plenty of time and coaxing, there was no response to that one either. I answered again in order to move on to my third question. When the same thing was happening, I said, "What's the matter with you people? I know you know the answers to these questions."

Silence.

Then I heard, "Brr, well close up!" from my wife.

I was speechless myself as I thought about an appropriate response. If my own wife thought I was doing that poorly, maybe I should give up.

"Shall we pray," I said, and then I closed the service in prayer.

Then it was Patricia's turn to be shocked. "Lee," she asked as I was coming down from the platform, "What is the matter?"

"Nothing," I replied. "You told me to close up, so I did."

The rest of the congregation was getting to their feet in relieved surprise.

"I did not tell you to close up!" Patricia declared. "What did you think I said?"

"You said, 'Well close up,' and I decided if I was doing that bad, maybe I should."

"I said we're froze up!" Patricia clarified.

We all had an embarrassed chuckle out of the situation, but there was no objection to going home.

How to Do Hospital Calling

Jim Crouch was a caring pastor who taught me a lot by his example. The first time he called on me in the hospital I was suffering from a serious problem with an ingrown toenail. Having difficulty hearing, Jim prayed for me loud enough to be able to hear himself. I am ashamed to say I was slightly embarrassed to have the whole hospital floor know he was praying so loudly for my big toe. Later, when I was again in the hospital in critical condition with hepatitis "A," I was so sick that I was glad to see him. I knew I needed help, and I didn't care how many people heard him. He had occasion to call on Patricia a couple of times as well and was equally comforting. Following his example, I have tried to be sensitive to others in their time of need and offer prayer when I have called on them in the hospital. I sense that most patients appreciate prayer, and I have witnessed some remarkable recoveries following prayer.

Lee R. Clendenning, PhD

The Rest of the Story

For a few years, we tried to keep up with the Lansing Friends Church as we moved from place to place. We took both of our sons back there for their baby dedications. We returned for the wedding of Jim's youngest daughter who had been a part of my Youth Class. She notified us that her mother had reconciled with her God before her death. We also returned to the church after Jim passed away. I pictured him entering the land of Beulah, which he loved to sing about, and hearing, "Well done, my good and faithful servant." Many years later we were in the Lansing area reminiscing and exploring changes in the community. We were surprised and pleased to find a new housing subdivision with a new church chapel; the sign in front read, "Crouch Memorial." At some point, the congregation was able to build their own, more modern place of worship.

Completing the BS Degree program

I continued to have a very successful college career. I was not interested in beer parties, so I avoided the Greek social scene. Patricia did manage to rid me of the "ain't" word. I developed more of the behavioral patterns of professional peers. Without seeking the office, I was nominated and then elected President of the College Industrial Arts Club. Mr. Loper's help in scheduling courses with majors in the math and science areas increased my exposure to a wider than normal range of faculty and their great students. I was invited, and joined, five academic honor societies, two in education, and one each in math, science, and industrial arts. I was named and listed in *Who's Who in American Colleges and Universities*. None of this would have been possible without Patricia's hard work, encouragement, management skills, and academic support typing my manuscripts and drilling me before tests. Her constant sacrifices inspired me to success.

Correcting Spoken Grammar

While student teaching in the fall semester of my senior year, I really determined that I needed to talk like a professional. After saying "were" in a lesson, I was interrupted by a little red-headed boy.

Mr. Clendenning, he said, "You are supposed to say "was" in a sentence like you just said."

"I'm sorry." I replied, "You are right." There were other corrections from other students as the semester continued. If I was going to be a professional educator, I did not need eighth graders correcting my speech.

Starting the final spring semester, I approached the Head of the English Department and explained my grammatical problems. I asked her if the English Department offered a serious formal grammar course. Of course, they did; she taught the course. The prerequisites were to be a senior English Teaching Major, with at least a "C" grade in all required major courses. Naturally, I had no such courses. I could see that a sales job was in order. I didn't need the hours for graduation. I had a grade point average high enough not to be bothered by a failing grade if it came to that. I promised I would not give her any trouble or make myself obnoxious in her class. Because I knew watered down courses for shop boys were a sore point among the academic elite of the college, I told her that the English classes I took as a shop boy were watered down, and I wanted a real English education. We compromised on approval for my enrollment with the understanding that we would both watch the date for honorable withdrawal, and either one of us could end the enrollment.

The class was a challenge. We reviewed the history of human languages, the families of languages and relationships among them. That is, the class reviewed; it was new material for me! Then we studied syntax, semantics, and the grammatical rules of formal English sentences with the meta-language descriptors of the functions and placement of key elements. We diagrammed sentences. My midterm and final grades were B's.

Again, the "Unseen Hand" was working. Later, as a PhD. candidate, I was able to use my fluency in computer languages in lieu of the foreign language requirement. This required that I demonstrate understanding of most of the concepts learned about languages in my course at Oswego. Every computer language has a carefully defined grammar, elements of syntax and semantics, and an equally carefully designed meta-language to explain the language to others. I have taught Berry College students how to develop, implement, and present their own original computer languages for personal or proprietary purposes.

Awarded an Assistanceship for Master's Degree studies

Like my contemporaries, I spent some time during the last semester preparing a resume, getting references on file in the College Placement Center, and interviewing for my first professional job. I had jumped through all the hoops, and I had a contract in hand to teach high school industrial arts for the City of Cortland, NY. Cortland was the closest system to my original home that offered industrial arts. The day that I was going to sign the contract and mail it to Cortland, I received a letter from Ohio University in Athens, Ohio, saying that I had been recommended by my Department Head for a graduate assistanceship to study there for a Master's Degree. The assistanceship paid a salary of $2,000 for half-time academic work with all fees and tuition waived for two summer terms and the academic year. There were papers for me to fill out and sign indicating my acceptance. I had never heard of a "Graduate Assistanceship" because Oswego State didn't use faculty assistants at the time I was there. Now I had one, and I would have been very excited if I had understood the honor better at the time.

I held both my Cortland contract and my offer from Ohio University as I went into the Department Head's office the next day. He had replaced the previous Department Head who had been upset with me as a freshman. He confirmed that he had sent my resume and placement references to the Department Head at Ohio University, where he had earned his own BS degree. He further explained that a graduate assistant was assigned to work half-time under the supervision of one or more regular professors doing whatever academic tasks the assistant could be trusted to perform. Many supervised students in laboratory assignments, some graded papers, tests, and/or projects. A few were even trusted to assume full responsibility for delivery of a course.

The Department Head had compelling arguments why an assistantship was an opportunity which I should not overlook at this point in my career. New York State required teachers to obtain a Master's degree within five years in order to keep their certification. Most completed the degree at their own expense through summer sessions; I could do it now in one year with the assistantship. The experience would look great on my resume. The State salary schedule was $1,000 higher at every step for teachers with a Master's degree, which would soon compensate for the low assistant's salary the first year. He also said that the University had very inexpensive married student housing.

The opportunity being dropped into my lap sounded too good to be true, but I was cautious. Patricia and I were expecting our first child in September. I called the Ohio University Department Head and set up an appointment to look over the Department and the area. While there, I also met the faculty and three current graduate assistants who would be graduating at the end of the up-coming summer session. Everyone was very friendly, patiently answering what I now know were elementary questions about the life and expectations of graduate assistants. Their shops were not as extensive in subject content or as big as those in Oswego, but what they did have were obviously well-maintained. Married student housing was cheap because it consisted of a series of old two-story army barracks, each divided into eight apartments. There seemed to be a sense of shared community. The University provided heat and utilities. There was a regularly scheduled bus service and shared solar drying lines for laundry.

Before we left, I accepted their offer, reserved an end apartment on a lower floor so that Patricia would not have to climb stairs carrying a baby, and established my class schedule for the summer term. They were to determine my work assignments in the fall.

Lee R. Clendenning, PhD

Opposition to Master's Degree studies

Neither Patricia's parents nor mine appreciated the opportunity I felt that the Lord had provided. Patricia's father took me down to the barn and gave me the only chewing out I ever got from him. Didn't I know that I had a pregnant wife? Didn't I know that it was my responsibility to support her and the baby? Didn't I know that a job in Cortland would keep her close to home and family? Hadn't she worked hard and long enough for me already? Didn't she deserve my taking a regular job instead of running off to Ohio for less than one half of the salary? (The Cortland offer was $4,800.) I had no real defense except that I sensed that this was God's will for us. The professional arguments would mean nothing to him.

My dad asked me if I was going to turn into a "Professional Student." He asked if I had joined "The Party" yet. I knew what he meant and assured him that I was not a card-carrying Communist.

"You will have to join if you stay in higher education," he predicted. Dad had a proposition for me. He wanted me to stay near home and he would deed the farm over to Andy and me, 50/50, while retaining life use of the property.

"What about my sisters and Dan?" I asked.

His reply was typical of him. "It's my property; I can do what I want with it."

I knew Dad, and I knew enough to smell a trap. I suspect what he really wanted was me on the hook for any repairs and expenses needed for the property from then on. In my mind, I could hear, "It's your place, the fence needs fixing, the pump needs replacement, taxes are due, etc, etc." I told him that I was going to Ohio. I did not know where I might go from there, but I would not be in a position either physically or financially to look after the property. If Andy wanted the farm, he could have it; he would earn anything he got out of it.

Dad was incredulous. "You would turn your back on your inheritance?" he demanded.

"Yes," I replied. "I will go my own way." I have never regretted that decision.

Chapter 11

1963-64, Master's Degree Program in Ohio

We had only ten days between my graduation at Oswego and classes beginning in Ohio. During that time, we sold the mobile home, losing only $500 in depreciation over the four years we had lived in it. We moved my personal shop machines to storage in Patricia's father's equipment barn, loaded our remaining possessions in a U-Haul trailer, and headed for Ohio.

The barracks apartment had cracks in the floorboards wide enough for us to see the ground, but also wide enough for big cockroaches to enter and exit at will. I found used rugs in second-hand stores, which Patricia called my "Lucky Day" shops, cleaned them, and covered up the cracks. I also picked up an old washing machine for the laundry and diapers. There were no Pampers back then. We started the process of finding a new church home by visiting a few smaller churches native to the region.

Summer classes, with all mature colleagues, were professionally valuable. In attendance were practicing teachers, the three outgoing graduate assistants, and we three new replacements. All of us and the entire Departmental faculty attended meetings sponsored by the industrial arts honorary fraternity where guest speakers presented topics of interest. Somehow, I was designated the corresponding secretary to send invitations and thank you letters to the presenters; more typing for Patricia.

Patricia wanted to return to home territory to have our baby in Syracuse Crouse Irving Hospital. We went home to Fabius, and Lee Roy Clendenning, Jr. was born September 11, 1963. I brought Patricia and Chip (Chip off the old block) to her parents home on a Sunday and had to leave for Ohio University Fall Registration on Monday. I left the car for Patricia and took the most lonely bus ride of my life to Ohio. After two weeks, I rode the same route in reverse to bring my family back to Ohio. Chip was an unbelievably good-natured baby. He slept most of the way back, and slept seven hours each night after we arrived. He definitely has been God's special gift to us.

Our search for a church home ended at a small Free Methodist congregation of local, country people. There were a number of unrelated families rather than one big clan like the folk at Lansing. The young pastor was in his final year of studies at Circleville Bible College, so he and his wife were in town only on Wednesdays and weekends. The folks adopted us as part of their group. The women would quibble with each other over who was going to hold Chip while Patricia played the piano. I was too busy to teach a Sunday school class, but Patricia taught a pre-school class. Occasionally, they were desperate enough to ask me to lead the singing. I did fill the pulpit once. I am thankful that this event was not as big a disaster as the cold night in Lansing. There were also enough young married couples to have a few enjoyable social events.

Over the course of the year in the Department, I assisted in all of the labs, but spent most of my time in the electronics area. I completed my Master's Thesis comparing the achievement of lab students working in different sized lab groups. I needed to calculate correlation coefficients between achievement quizzes and group sizes after every lab session. Without a scientific calculator, or computer spread sheet, this was a formidable task. Luckily for me, as a professional bookkeeper, Patricia was a whiz at basic manual number crunching. I "programmed" her to do the calculations as I fed her the data. I came to the grand conclusion that good students do well in any sized group, while weak students do poorly regardless of the group size.

Where is the computer?

While my peers in the Master's program, hoping to be principals someday, all minored in Educational Administration, I had to be different and minor in Mathematics. I had no desire to be a public school principal, and little did I know that years later I would need those graduate math hours to satisfy Berry College's accreditation requirements for teaching in their Mathematics and Computer Science Department!

One course I took in the Ohio University Mathematics Department was Digital Computer Programming. We studied the binary number system, how to represent numbers and do arithmetic using 2's complement representations, and machine language programming. I kept waiting to see and touch this new, exciting machine called a computer.

One day I asked the professor, "When do we get to see the computer?"

"You will not," he answered. "I understand there is one on campus somewhere, but I haven't actually seen it myself."

Remember, this was 1964. We submitted our programs to the professor on notebook paper. He analyzed the program code to decide whether it would run or not if properly submitted to a real computer. I was glad I was not his assisting grader! I did not get near a real computer until 1969 during my doctorate program.

Assassination, flood, and the "War onPoverty"

There were three very memorable events during our stay in Ohio. First, I was sitting in a barber's chair listening to the background music as my hair was cut when there was an interrupting announcement. President John F. Kennedy was shot as his motorcade passed a grassy knoll in Dallas, Texas. (The first reports that the shots came from the grassy knoll were later refuted.) We, along with the nation, were stunned. Second, the following spring the Ohio University campus was flooded by the Hocking River, backed up by the record Ohio River flood. For up-land people like us, it was a real sight to see motorboats cruising down the airport runway. We took back roads over the mountain to get a birds-eye view of the Ohio River filling its valley. Trees, houses, and other debris moved at terrific speed toward the Mississippi. Third, Athens and Ohio University were the hosts to President Johnson when he declared "War on Poverty." After some cleanup from the flood, President Johnson announced he was coming to Athens. Everybody thought he was coming to inspect flood damage. I soon realized that he was not addressing the audience in front of him, but the rest of the nation via television. In days to follow, as his war progressed, first, it was only Athens County in Ohio and four other counties in adjoining West Virginia and Kentucky that were poor. But, we soon learned that poverty was infecting the entire Appalachian region, and then it was discovered throughout the whole country. As they say, the rest is history. His speech is recorded in the Lyndon B. Johnson Library: (http://www.presidency.ucsb.edu/ws/index.php?pid=26225#axzz1uhZx2MTT)

Moving back to New York

Over Easter Vacation, we returned to Fabius to seek a teaching position near home. The East Syracuse-Minoa School system had a new high school under construction, and they were looking for an industrial arts teacher, primarily to teach electronics. I lined up an interview and had the job nailed down before returning to Ohio. The salary was $5,800, so I was vindicated for my decision to accept the Ohio Assistanceship.

I finished all requirements for my Master's Degree in Industrial Arts Education at the end of the first summer term, but could not afford to stay in Ohio to attend graduation ceremonies. We moved back to New York and found a suitable house to rent on the edge of the village of Kirkville, New York, about four miles from the school where I would be teaching. Construction of the new high school was way behind schedule, so I was reassigned to the old Minoa Junior/Senior High School. My revised teaching assignments included multiple sections of Junior High woodworking and one Senior High electronics class. I also was to supervise one study hall. I was eager to start my new professional career.

Chapter 12

1964-1965, Public School Teaching and Parental Care

I really enjoyed public school teaching after I was able to create a teaching schedule which met the needs of all my students. At the time, the school was committed to ability grouping of the student body, but was using the concept of "mainstreaming" students with special needs into the enrichment courses such as industrial arts. The two or three special needs boys who were mainstreamed into each of the industrial arts classes were totally lost. (Girls did not take industrial arts back then.) One tall boy didn't want anybody to see his body, so he spent his time crouched behind a work table. Looking over the lab during work time, I would spot just his forehead eyes and nose keeping track of me. Two other boys had obvious Down's syndrome. I knew immediately that something had to change to meet any of these "special needs."

The only period of the day which I dreaded was the supervision of study hall. The administrative rule was that students were only allowed to leave the room in a dire emergency. Restroom breaks were to be limited to one at a time of each gender. I had to play sergeant in issuing passes to band practice, conferences with other teachers, dental appointments, and any other reasons students had, or invented, in an attempt to leave the room.

I decided to try to solve both of my problems at once. I described to the Principal how I could help the special needs students if I could get all eight of them into a class of their own. There were manipulative hand and eye coordination exercises that could be tailored to benefit even the Down's syndrome students. He liked the possibilities.

Then he observed, "It wouldn't be fair to you to take on an extra class, you have a full load already."

BINGO! "I would be happy to do it during the time I now watch study hall," I offered, "if you could find someone else for that period."

He thought a minute. "I can do that," he said. "Let's start Monday morning."

The Special Education teacher was also happy with the idea; talk about "Win, Win!"

With a few bumps in the road, the idea to serve the special needs students separately worked out fine. I spent the weekend after my conference with the principal planning for the first class session. I carved shallow bowl and ashtray-shaped hollows in the top of heavy wooden blocks. I had flat aluminum sheet metal disks to cover the depressions. When the special needs students came in, I set them to hammering dents into the top of the aluminum. They thought it was great fun. The Down's syndrome boys looked at the floor, the ceiling, and out of the window, as they pounded away. As some of the other students saw the metal start to take the shape I had carved into the blocks, they began pounding with more purpose. At the end of the period, I stopped the Down's students and asked them to look at what they had been hammering.

They looked amazed! "Where did that bowl come from?" one asked bewilderedly.

"You made it!" I replied.

"Can I have it?"

"Sure, take it home."

"Can we make another one tomorrow?" The tall one had come out of hiding.

"Yes! Let's all make one more," I said.

I wanted them to show other students, teachers, and parents what they had done, and they didn't disappoint me. Word spread fast to the whole school. Initial successes in their first projects led to a great year.

The ceramic working equipment in my shop was not directly needed to teach my assigned subjects. However, I used the kiln, a potter's wheel, and a wide selection of slip-cast molds to good advantage. I showed my special needs students how to make professional looking pieces using the molds. They liked working with clay.

A new church home

Meanwhile, we found a new church home with a small Wesleyan Methodist congregation meeting in the basement of a building under construction about two miles north of our home in Kirkville. The group included mostly young couples starting families like us and the pastor and his wife, who were parents of school age boys. The pastor was also a counselor in the school system. By Christmas time, I was providing youth leadership for the few teenagers that attended. The pastor and his wife were very supportive of us as we went through the remainder of Patricia's pregnancy and unexpected medical complications with our new baby, Richard Bruce Clendenning, another blessing from God. We lost track of the pastor's family in the next few years, but in a later return visit to the area, we were pleased to see that the new worship center had been completed.

Caring for My Parents

Serious medical problems had forced major changes in the life of my parents. Mother had been diagnosed with breast cancer and was now participating in medical research trials sponsored by the State Cancer Research Center at Buffalo, NY. Dad had also been diagnosed with serious heart disease. Dad, Mother, and Dan, who was ten years old, had given up living on the home farm and moved to live with Sylvia's family in Scotia, NY.

When we started living in Kirkville, we were about midway between Sylvia's home and Mother's treatment center, so the family expected that we would provide much of the transportation and care during recovery between treatments. Not being employed, Dad accompanied Mother wherever she went. Dad had strong opinions on every aspect of life which he could not keep to himself. As Patricia was recovering from a difficult delivery, caring for a new baby requiring surgery, and dealing with Chip's unexpected sickness, the burden of caring for ungrateful and intrusive in-laws was more than I should have asked of her. I tried to help her by caring for Richard through the night, but, I wasn't home through the day. I really should have been hard-nosed and demanded that my sisters share more of the load. At the time, I strongly felt that my responsibility as a son was to provide for the care of my parents. I promised Patricia that if, and whenever, her parents needed care, I would be there for her and them (That time came years later). The ultimate irony was that my sisters apparently believed Dad's complaints that Patricia was not a submissive wife. This false accusation against her created unnecessary animosity toward her from my sisters for years to come. We searched and found a bigger house that would accommodate separate living quarters for us and my parents with Dan. Dad was with me at the final meeting with the real estate broker, approved the home, and even put up $100 cash earnest money to hold the property. I was the only one to sign the sales contract.

Another surprise opportunity

Again, the "Unseen Hand" was working behind the scenes to bring an end to my current family problems while providing a new opportunity for me. The school system had a strict policy against personal phone calls and had made it clear they would not put through such calls. However, one morning, another voice over the intercom said, "Mr. Clendenning, come to the office. You have a long distance call from New Jersey." As I walked to the office, I couldn't think of anyone I might know in New Jersey.

The call was from a professor whom I had assisted in Ohio the previous year. After I left Ohio, he had accepted a position with Montclair State College in New Jersey, and had been there while I was in Minoa. Their electronics instructor had just resigned, and they were looking for a replacement. If I wanted the job, he had authorization to mail me a contract. This was before the days when such positions had to be nationally advertised. I made an appointment to visit the College immediately. My parents left for a temporary visit to Andy's home. We arranged for Patricia's parents to watch Chip and Richard in our absence and prayed about the situation.

What should I do? I was committed to buy a home for two families. It seemed like my obligation to my parents was more important than my new opportunity. Just before we left for the interview, we learned that Dad had changed his mind about living with us. He wanted his $100 back to help with the purchase of a mobile home so he could live in a park near Andy.

On our visit to Montclair State College, we found that the laboratory facilities included one massive comprehensive general shop which could accommodate different classes in different activities simultaneously. There were also separate facilities for drafting, electronics, and classroom lecturing. I would be expected to teach a mixed load of electronics, drafting, and graphic arts/printing classes. They had a contract for me to sign offering a salary of $6,800. Then the Department Head said, "By the way, the President will need an application from you before you leave." They found an empty desk with a typewriter, and Patricia typed the application as I gave her the information requested as best I could from immediate memory. When I was interviewed by the President, I learned he was a much earlier graduate of Oswego. After some small talk, he looked at our makeshift application.

"Oh, I see you were inducted into *Who's Who*. That's good," he said. One never knows what will attract an evaluator's attention.

My former professor from Ohio University and his wife acted as hosts to our visit, providing lodging and a narrated tour of the area. The day was clear enough for us to see the George Washington Bridge and New York skyline from campus. While we were so close to New York City, we visited the 1965 World's Fair. Quite bedazzling for us country folk!

Back home, I had to do something about the sales contract for the house. I contacted the sellers, explained my situation, and offered a generous settlement to cancel the contract. I was sure they could find another buyer. They rejected my offer and threatened a breach of contract lawsuit if I backed out. I wanted to do the right thing. I then contacted a lawyer, and on his advice, left the matter in his hands. He was able to find discrepancies in the history of the deed which got me off the hook. By being hard-nosed, the sellers lost the money I was willing to pay them. On the other hand, I was protected from buying property with an improper title.

During the summer, we had to plan our move to Montclair. We went to New Jersey again and found an apartment. Patricia's father knew a man with a large truck which he said would be ideal for our move. When the time came, we discovered that the truck had commonly been used for transporting bulk coal! The owner assured us that he had a big canvas covering to keep our goods dry in case of rain. After loading, we drove ahead to prepare the apartment for our home furnishings.

The previous tenants had left the apartment totally trashed and unclean. I always had a weak stomach; I made the mistake of inhaling as I opened the refrigerator door. The rancid odor was so bad that I lost my lunch immediately. Patricia was a stoic trooper while cleaning and disinfecting the mess.

Meanwhile, rain poured into the truck which arrived long after dark with our wet household items. We unloaded and spread out our belongings to dry as best we could. Our new life in New Jersey had begun.

Chapter 13

Life in New Jersey— Montclair State College

For country folk, life in metropolitan New Jersey was an educational challenge. We had to learn how to navigate in the horrendous traffic and cope with different cultural expectations. Taking the children for a walk with the stroller one day, Patricia was stopped by a well-meaning local woman. Patricia was told that what she was doing was very unsafe. She could be mugged and/or the children kidnapped. Apparently due to lack of trust or fear, people kept to themselves and took care of only their own families. One time, I was pushing Chip in a swing in a small public park. The little girl in the swing next to him called, "Mommy, come push me." Without thinking about it, I shifted to the left and gave the girl a couple of gentle pushes. The mother came right over, gave me a dirty look as if I were a pervert, took the girl in her arms and left the park. I knew that nothing I could say would alleviate that mother's fears. At a church picnic, everyone sat with their families and brought all provisions they individually needed. There was no common table. When we asked, "Does anybody have some salt?" We heard one person mutter, "If they wanted salt, why didn't they bring it?" At the same picnic, Patricia started to pass around a cake that she had baked. It took a little bit of coaxing to convince them that we really meant to share the cake. Finally, one man said, "It sure looks good. I am going to have a piece." Then others followed. They were good people, just raised in a different culture.

Finding a church that would let us keep Chip and Richard during the service took a while. We had never attended anyplace sophisticated enough to have a nursery. They were our babies, and we were not about to trust their care to total strangers. Generally, church ushers quietly tried to direct us to the nursery, but one time, we sneaked into the back row of a church. Someone went to the microphone and announced over the loudspeaker, "Please take your children to the nursery. The usher will show you where it is." We already knew where the exit door was, and we left. We finally found a small Christian and Missionary Alliance Church that would allow us to sit in the back row with our boys, even though they really didn't like it. Patricia played the piano for them and also for a monthly singspiration with other churches, and for the jail ministry. I taught the junior boys class and spoke a couple of times at the jail.

Seeing the Sights

While in the metropolitan area, I finally grew brave enough to drive in New York City and decided to take advantage of some of the well-known attractions. When Andy and family came for a visit, we went to Coney Island. Later, Patricia and I walked around in Central Park and visited the Empire State Building. At that time, Rita and her family were living in Riverhead, Long Island, so we visited them and the ocean beach there. Evelyn visited on a day that I had to go to Bayonne Naval Base in New Jersey to pick up some surplus material. We were pleasantly surprised to come over a hill top on the New Jersey Turnpike Extension and look the Statue of Liberty square in the face. We visited the Turtle Park Zoo, near Montclair, where the attraction was monstrous turtles.

One Saturday, we decided to try what was touted to be the most enjoyable outing for a Montclair family, a trip to the Jersey Shore. Never again! The trip was over four hours of bumper-to-bumper traffic on the Garden State Parkway, a toll road which required stops every few miles to throw coins in a toll booth in order to continue. It seemed like everybody in the northern end of the State was doing the same thing.

Once there, we found the sea breeze so brutal that heavy beach umbrellas were set up as wind shields rather than sun shields. Chip and Rick could not stand to be out of the car. We and a few million others headed for home, another four-hour drive. We had all the fun we could stand!

The Swamps of Secausus were unpleasant distractions in the region. Unfortunately, they were still being used as a garbage dump for the whole Newark, New Jersey, and New York City metropolitan area. The dump fires added to the choking smog and the awful odor. Many places we wanted to go required driving fifteen to twenty miles through that area. The Manhattan skyline was often obscured because of the smoke from the dumps.

Teaching at Montclair State College

At the time I was teaching there, Montclair State had a philosophy for controlling student academic quality opposite to that of Oswego. The faculty were told repeatedly, "We are very selective in whom we accept. Approximately 80% of the students are high school valedictorians." The clear implication was if students were not performing well in class, it was probably the fault of the faculty. I had no problems in the drafting and graphic arts classes. However, other students saw no reason to learn the required basic electronics when they were sure they would never teach it. I noticed a lackadaisical attitude toward performing the laboratory exercises. So, I gave them a surprise quiz. They were unconcerned when half of them failed. I asked what they thought was the problem.

"We don't have to learn this stuff," was their answer.

I reminded them that the course was required in the curriculum. They replied that they did not design or approve the curriculum. To no avail, I explained that their certification as industrial arts teachers covered electronics; someday they might be assigned to teach the course. I finally resorted to the professor's ultimate threat: "If you don't learn it, I will have to fail you."

They just laughed. "This is Montclair," they said. "Nobody flunks here!"

"But you will give me no other choice," I countered.

"You are a new professor," one answered. "You will not dare flunk all of us."

I conceded, "You are right, but you will have to gamble on how many I do dare fail."

As the semester progressed, attendance in the electronics lectures was weak and lab times were squandered. Half of the class failed the mid-term exam, again with no concern. By the end of the semester, I knew in this institution I would need a convincing standard to apply to those that failed. I made up a very basic final exam with a few circuit analysis problems which would clearly be right or wrong and factual multiple choice questions with indisputable answers. I submitted my handwritten script to the Departmental Secretary for typing and duplicating. I asked her, "Have you ever studied electronics?"

She, of course, answered, "No, I have only typed tests like I just did for you."

"Good," I said. "I want you to take this test." She thought I was crazy, but I convinced her that I needed her to take the test and do her best.

After administering the test to the class, I failed the seven students who did not score as well as the secretary. There was a howl of protest! The Department Head called me in to discuss student complaints.

After review of the test, he asked, "How did you establish the passing grade?"

"I asked the Secretary to take the test. I failed anyone who could not do as well as someone who had never studied the course."

He thought a minute; then he said, "It is a sign of a good teacher when you have the courage to uphold your standards. You will have to explain what you did to the Dean and probably the President."

He was right; I had to explain my actions at those levels. I survived the crisis. The following semester, I had seven serious believers in my class to convince the new enrollees that I meant business.

The Beginning of grade Inflation

In the 1960s, the Vietnam War required the US Government to greatly expand the military draft to raise the necessary manpower.

The draft system was using good college grades as criteria for granting school deferments. One of our students, who received failing grades in June, was drafted, completed basic training, deployed, and killed before Christmas. I am thankful he was not one I had failed. Many professors took the position that someone else would have to pick who should live and who should die. So there was pressure to inflate grades. In the next few years, as the resistance to the Vietnam War strengthened, the increased pressure to inflate grades was felt across the country. Eventually, the Congress changed the deferment policy, but grades never settled back to the old standards.

Industrial Internship at Western Electric Corp

Late in the spring of 1966, the Community Relations Officer of Western Electric Company contacted Montclair's Department Head and offered paid summer internships in their New Jersey operations for two students and a supervising instructor. Western Electric was the manufacturing arm of the big telephone company, AT&T. Their goal was "To increase the industrial awareness of industrial arts teachers." Accepting the offer, I recruited two of my best students, and we spent the summer studying first-hand how a massive manufacturing facility operated. Company managers took us on tours of related facilities like the Bell Telephone Laboratories, the Long Lines Antenna Farm which carried communications across the ocean, the wire making plant, and the Instrument Calibration Department. Montclair granted undergraduate credit to my students, while I was able to enroll for graduate credit through Trenton State College. The internship was a grand eye-opening experience for a country boy, allowing me to understand the realities of large scale industrial practices.

Mother Lost Her Battle

My mother lost her battle with breast cancer in the spring of 1966. Toward the end, she said that if she had known how she would suffer through the experimental procedures and operations she had endured, she would have taken her chances with the disease and never gone near the New York Cancer Center in Buffalo. Her suffering was not totally in vain; pioneers like her helped researchers sort out what helps or does not help others. She spent her last few months being cared for by my sister Dawn in Endwell, New York.

Escape from racial unrest and old technology

Two developments led to the decision to leave New Jersey. During the winter and spring of 1967, there was growing racial unrest in the Newark, New Jersey area, as well as other big cities. Civil rights leaders held rallies very near our apartment building. I sensed that "spontaneous riots" were going to break out in the near future, and I became apprehensive about the safety of my family. During this same period, the electronic world was switching from vacuum tube to transistor (solid state) technology. All my electronic training was with vacuum tubes. Being concerned that the college lab and instrumentation was becoming obsolete because they were vacuum tube based, I requested funds to purchase some transistor based training equipment. This request was denied with little promise of approval in the near future.

I attended the International Conference of the American Industrial Arts Association in Philadelphia, PA, in late spring. Many of the sessions dealt with meeting the challenge of switching instruction to solid state electronics in industrial arts teacher education programs. At every conference, the Association sponsored a booth devoted to matching posted job openings with potential applicants. One posting from Stout State University in Menomonie, Wisconsin, attracted my attention:

"Electronic Instructor competent to teach, <u>OR WILLING TO LEARN TO TEACH</u> solid state electronics" (Emphasis mine).

I knew Stout State had the second largest program of industrial arts teacher education in the world. I scheduled an interview with Stout's Dean of the School of Technology who was attending the conference. We developed an almost instant rapport. I was honest about my complete lack of expertise in solid state electronics, but I was sure I could stay ahead of the students in learning as I taught. He offered me the job and I accepted on the spot.

I was eager to share the news of my new position with Patricia, but New Jersey Bell was having a strike of telephone workers. It was 3:00 a.m. when I was finally connected to Patricia. I guess she had been married to me long enough not to be shocked at anything I did. When I asked her how she would like to move to Wisconsin, she sleepily replied, "I guess that would be OK, if you are sure that is what you want to do." And my family had accused her of not being a submissive wife!

I want out of metropolitan New Jersey!

In the spring of 1967, as the semester was drawing to a close, the racial tensions in Newark were spreading to the suburbs, and my apprehensions regarding the safety of my family increased. I called the Department Chair at Stout State, whom I had never met, and asked him if there was any possibility of summer work and immediate housing if I moved there at the start of the summer instead of the end.

"Sure," he replied without hesitation. "Come on out! There is a campus ministry house your family can live in long enough to find other quarters. I can find you a summer job in a local electronics industry."

Praise the Lord! We moved just two weeks before twenty-six people were killed and over one hundred injured in the Newark riots.

CHAPTER 14

LIFE AND TEACHING IN WISCONSIN—STOUT STATE UNIVERSITY

In preparation for our move, I traded in our compact 1962 Ford Falcon station wagon for a small Dodge van. I wanted a more rugged vehicle to pull a U-Haul trailer and one with more space to accommodate the growing children. I constructed a false floor in the rear, elevated enough to hold suitcases and a layer of boxes beneath it. A mattress on the floor provided a play and sleeping area. This was before seat belt laws. We loaded up, stopped briefly in Fabius to visit family and reorganize, and then headed for the unknown adventure of Wisconsin.

Menomonie, Wisconsin was a quiet-college town wrapped around one side of a lake that had been created by a small power dam on a nearby river. The most traffic occurred on Friday afternoons and evenings when dairy farmers from the surrounding area came to town for supplies. Stout State University was the only major employer. In days gone by, Menomonie had been the center of a lumbering industry. The openness and cleanness of the environment was a welcome relief from the closed in atmosphere of metropolitan New Jersey. The town and the campus were small enough for one to walk easily or ride a bicycle to any place of interest. We found the small campus ministry cottage and met my new Department Chair.

The Department Chair had arranged for me to work in the home laboratories of National Presto Industries in Eau Claire, thirty miles from Menomonie. He had even arranged for me to carpool with other people working there so that our vehicle could be left with Patricia through the day. National Presto Industries manufactured small home appliances such as toasters, blenders, mixers, hair driers, pressure cookers, and electric flat irons. They put national retailers' labels, such as Sears and J C Penny, on many of the products as they were made, but also sold products under their own brand. The Laboratories were charged with the responsibility of troubleshooting returned products for defects, investigating damage claims for personal accidents involving company products, and researching and developing new products. The latter function was my assignment. I worked with people holding the original patents on such things as the electric tooth brush and hair drier. I was assigned to design, assemble, and demonstrate a battery charger without using an expensive and heavy transformer. I also developed a timer for inclusion in a kitchen blender. I had to use solid state devices in these assignments, so my solid state studies began with real practical problems. I was being paid for preparation for my fall classes.

God provides our own home

Apart from work, the first item on our agenda was to find more permanent housing. Between married students and young faculty, there was little vacant housing available. In a small town, people know each other and their business. One of my new faculty friends knew somebody with a house for rent. When we went to look at it, the house had streets on three sides and no outdoor play yard. Upon our rejection of this rental property, the potential landlords, a middle-aged couple, described their personal residence which was also for sale. If we would look at it, maybe a deal could be worked out. I was sure there was no way we could afford a house. But at their insistence, we agreed to go look.

As we arrived, we saw a "For Sale by Owner" sign in front of a full, two-story, older home with a back yard. The house was not really run down, but it obviously was in need of routine maintenance. Inside, the house had minimal modernization. There was a flush toilet and a shower stall. The good-sized kitchen had an old-fashioned, single basin sink, one wall cabinet, and very little counter space. There was a gas water heater and central heating system.

The owners explained that in Wisconsin, they could sell us the property on a "Land Contract" that would not involve a bank or a mortgage, closing costs, or a big down payment. Monthly payments, including interest on the unpaid principle, would be no more than rent would cost us anywhere else. The property would be ours to maintain, or improve to suit ourselves as long as we kept making payments to them until the sale price was satisfied. The legal arrangement sounded too good to be true, especially since I could do my own carpentry, plumbing, and electrical work at my own speed. We met with their lawyer who confirmed everything they had claimed, drew up the contract, provided a payment schedule, and witnessed our signatures. I know today as I write this, it sounds like a flim-flam deal; but time proved them to be honest people.

I had been in Wisconsin less than three weeks, and the Lord had provided temporary housing, a summer job with carpool to get to work which also was preparing me for fall classes, and now a permanent home. Nobody could be that lucky! My cup ran over!

Tornadoes and Cold!

Even when compared to upstate New York, weather was the most surprising change for us. The first surprise came late Friday evening of the third week we were in Menomonie. While I was outside talking with my new neighbor, a fellow faculty member, suddenly, there was a rushing of wind as the sky turned dark. Without saying a word, he turned and started running for his house. "That is sure strange behavior," I thought, as I watched him disappear. I went into our cottage and told Patricia about his action. Then there was real howling from outdoors. I went outside, and looked in the direction of the most noise, which sounded like a freight train passing just to the north. A terrible rain with heavy lightning and thunder forced me back inside. We lost power, but it was restored by morning.

By daylight the big yard around the cottage was covered with small tree branches with green leaves clinging. It was a mess! This was the day I was to move into our own house, so Patricia cleaned up the yard as I began the move. Our neighbor came over to be sure we were all right. He said that a tornado had struck just north of town. We had heard of tornadoes like the terrible storm in the *Wizard of Oz*, but the thought that we might ever experience one had never occurred to us. My neighbor was shocked by my stupid innocence.

"Didn't you take cover when I ran for home last night?" he asked.

"No," I answered, "I guess I didn't recognize the danger signs."

On the way to work Monday morning, I witnessed areas of unbelievable devastation. We had many close encounters with tornadoes during the years we lived in Wisconsin and Illinois, but the Lord always protected us from injury or real damage.

The winters were also colder and longer than anything we had experienced. During one three week stretch, the temperature did not rise above zero degrees, even in the heat of the day. The lake froze hard enough to support an ice fishing village complete with streets for car traffic. They held a stock car race on the ice. Parking for spectators' vehicles and even a Grey Hound bus were all supported on the ice. Surprisingly, the wind was usually quite gentle, so one did not notice the chill factor as much as in other places we had lived.

Teaching at Stout State University

Teaching at Stout State University was one of my most enjoyable professional experiences. Administratively, the School of Technology was sub-divided into academic departments by technical area. The Department of Electronics had its own Department Head. I was one of four professors, part of a very congenial and professional group, teaching electronics exclusively. The instructional labs were relatively new and very well-furnished for both vacuum tube and solid state technologies. My students were serious about the subjects and eager to learn. The solid state course was the most challenging. I will have to admit that the first time I taught it, there were a couple of days that I let the class go early because I had taught them all I knew.

Keeping the faith

We learned that Menomonie was Lutheran territory with a few other churches. The first year, we worked with one holiness church carrying a nationally recognized denominational title. The congregation was a mixture of middle class town folk and small family farmers. Patricia worked in the music program and the younger children's classes. I was drafted to teach a college and career class. There were enough other young couples to enjoy fellowship activities.

Enjoyable Sports

The opportunity to be an active spectator and supporter of sports teams sponsored by an institution is one of the benefits of college teaching. In the fall, we watched our first college football game at Stout. Stout also had a competitive basketball team. Chip had gotten old enough to enjoy the cheering, refreshments, and general excitement of going to the games with us. Richard was just taken along. Admission for faculty and their families was free, so attending games was one way to have an inexpensive family outing on cold Friday nights.

Foreign Students from Africa

During the second semester, a group of four students from somewhere in Africa appeared in my Electronics II class. One of them had scars on his cheeks like cat's whiskers, apparently made from cuts in a rite of passage ritual. They seemed to understand English when I spoke to them, but were reluctant to respond verbally to any question I asked. They followed the laboratory manual in the lab sessions and seemed to handle the instruments all right. The first test required some circuit analysis and written definitions of technical terms. Looking at their test papers, the only thing I could recognize was the question numbers before each response. I took the papers to the Department Chair for his advice.

He looked them over, then looked up at me with a pleasant expression and asked, "Can you say for sure that their responses are wrong?"

After some thought, I replied; "Well no, I can't. Maybe in whatever language they are using, they are correct."

Then he explained, "Look, Stout has a contract with the Department of State in Washington, DC, to provide technical training for these students. Their countries send us the most promising students they have. If they fail here, they will probably commit suicide rather than go home in disgrace. Unless you can show them exactly where they are wrong so that they can learn from their mistakes, just give them a 'Passing' grade. They will not question it."

Time proved that giving my African students the benefit of the doubt was a wise decision. By the end of the semester, I had established better rapport with them, and they had sufficient mastery of English to start submitting readable assignments and tests. I lost track of three of them after leaving Stout, but one of them remained in this country. He completed a PhD, and the last I heard of him, he was a college professor in Florida.

National Science Foundation Institute

During the spring semester, the National Science Foundation sent out an announcement of an institute in electronics and advanced mathematics for engineering technology instructors. The institute was to be offered by the General Engineering Department of the University of Illinois during the summer of 1968. A support stipend and all fees and tuition for graduate credit were available for accepted participants. The Department Head recommended that I apply. I filled out the application, sent it in, and received an acceptance letter back in short order. I also received information from the Institute Director regarding housing availability, and procedures for graduate credit. The plans for the coming summer and my in-service professional development were in place with minimal expense to me. I moved the family to a small apartment in Champaign, Illinois, for the summer.

My Institute classes covered advanced mathematical applications of matrix algebra to problems of circuit analysis. We also studied advanced applications of electromagnetism. Guest speakers were invited to present topics which might be of interest. I found the studies very difficult. The home work exercises and cramming for tests required late night work sessions.

One morning during the last week of the Institute, Dr. Shockley, a researcher at Bell Telephone Laboratories and co-inventor of the transistor, was an invited speaker. I was so excited to hear how he developed the transistor that I took a front row seat right under his nose with my pen and notepad. He was a monotone speaker. Suddenly, I heard my pen clatter to the floor. The problem was that I had burned the midnight oil doing assignments too many nights in a row. I was terribly embarrassed to have fallen asleep right in front of what should have been the most interesting lecture of my career. I picked up my pen without looking him in the eye and started to pretend to take notes. After some time, "Clickity Clatter!" It was my pen again. This time I was too embarrassed to retrieve it. I just got up and left as hurriedly as possible. Ever since, I have had a little more sympathy for students who have gone to sleep in my classes.

Another guest speaker at the Institute was a representative of the Department of Vocational-Technical and Adult Education at the University. He described their doctorate program as an opportunity for those who wanted to make a permanent career of college teaching. Without fully understanding why at the time, I recorded his title and address.

While we participants were involved in classes or collaborative studying, Patricia fellowshipped with some of the other spouses and looked after Chip and Richard. I bought her a small, portable radio/television to help pass the time. To occupy their time, she also took the boys to every Vacation Bible School program in the area and to a public park.

Old prejudices drives us to new ministries

When we returned to Wisconsin to start our second year, we discovered that our church had changed pastors. Unfortunately, the new pastor brought with him all the anti-education attitudes and rhetoric which I had experienced in my youth. When he said loudly from the pulpit that an educated man cannot know or follow the will of God, we realized that we needed to find a new church home. Giving up friendships that we had developed was difficult. In the meantime, the Christian and Missionary Alliance organization had started a new church in the area. Our long history with the Alliance made transition there a reasonably natural decision.

I also accepted a request to be Faculty Advisor to the Intervarsity Christian Fellowship, a small group of students on campus that enjoyed fellowship and singing. They organized themselves into a choir with Patricia as their pianist. We traveled to the students' hometowns giving short concerts in their churches.

How do I make a living?

The late 1960s were a time of very high economic inflation when prices and expenses suddenly rose much faster than faculty salaries. For Patricia and me, long-deferred dental care became urgent. There just wasn't enough salary to cover expenses. We had always tithed even in the thinnest of times, but our current situation really tested our commitment to charitable giving. As we were struggling to stay solvent, one of the Home Economics professors asked us if we would cooperate in a case study of family budgeting. She wanted to be able to present a realistic example of budgeting to her classes. We agreed to provide information as long as we were not personally identified. After going over our income and expenses with a fine tooth comb, she concluded, "I have no recommendations to improve your budgeting. You folks cannot make it!" She was not telling us something we didn't already know!

It was clear to us that we would have to do something to survive economically. We prayed. Then Patricia started selling Fuller Brush products part-time to balance the budget and keep food on the table. I met with my Department Head.

"How can I make a living teaching in college with the mismatch between salaries and rising expenses?" I asked.

He replied, "Lee, you are doing a wonderful job for us. We are really well pleased with your work, but, if you want to stay in college teaching and make money enough to support a family, you will have to get a doctorate." He also suggested that I ask for a leave of absence for the next academic year in order to start the course work for the doctorate.

Setting out to fulfill the Department Head's advice, I wrote to the technical education professor at the University of Illinois who had made the recruiting presentation at the NSF Institute. I reminded him of the NSF session, described my professional situation, and asked for admissions literature. He replied with a Graduate Catalog, Admission Form, and instructions to take the *Miller Analogies Test*. He also requested an example of my formal academic writing beyond my Master's Thesis or college term papers. I had not written any journal articles at this point in my career.

Talking with an older colleague clarified what I had to do. As a graduate of the University of Illinois doctorate program, he strongly suggested that I use a review book for the Miller test, and that I write a formal review of a serious educational philosophy book. He said that the Miller test was full of analogies, for example: Cat is to Calf as Dog is to _____, followed by four choices, none of which may make sense at the first glance. He said that without a prep book, I would never think of many of the possible relationships.

So, on a Saturday morning we went to the bookstore at the University of Minnesota in Minneapolis to pick up the Miller review book and select a book for my report. I chose a book on existentialism in educational thought, although I cannot remember or find the title on the web today. This was real heavy stuff for a shop boy! I wrote my report, Patricia typed it, and I sent it. I studied the review book for the Miller test and reported to the University of Minnesota to take the test.

The test score was sent directly to the University Of Illinois Graduate School Of Education. I soon received a letter announcing that I was tentatively accepted, pending a personal interview with the Head of my major department. With that letter in hand, I formally requested and was granted a year's leave of absence from Stout.

Chapter 15

PhD. Studies— University of Illinois, Urbana

During Spring Break of 1969, Patricia and I travelled with the boys to the University of Illinois for my personal interview with the Department Head and to explore housing possibilities. The interview went well except for one major change in my plans. The Department had made a decision to accept only truly serious students, committed to stay enrolled in the program the full two years until completion. If I were ready to sign that commitment, I would be accepted. I only had a leave of absence for one year, and I had told Patricia that she would only need to work for one year. I turned these things over in my mind as the Department Head waited for my decision. Finally, I thought, "Lord, I have come too far to back out now." I signed the papers, shook his hand, and went out to the van to face Patricia. Without saying anything, I drove to a more quiet side street and parked.

"Lee, what is the matter?" She demanded once, then twice.

"I had to make a commitment for two years in order to be accepted."

"Oh, is that all?"

"You don't understand. I'll have to stay here two years without an income. We have only made plans for one year."

She looked me right in the eye and said, "If we can survive one year, we can figure out how to survive two."

"Lord, what did I do to deserve such a good, supportive wife?" I thought as a wave of relief and confidence overtook me.

God directs and provides our housing

To achieve the second purpose of our journey, we had to seek housing. The Married Student Housing Office at the University had a long waiting list, so we explored the possibilities of a mobile home. We discovered that April was the wrong time of year for buying a used unit as most graduate students finished in August. We couldn't wait for the market because I started classes in June. With inflation approaching 15% a year, a dealer convinced us we could get most of our money back from a new mobile home in two years. The idea was to rent our Menomonie home to make the payments on a mobile unit. The sales contract was ready for my signature when I had a stroke of caution. Big decisions were happening too fast for my comfort zone.

"Let me take the papers with me and think about this. I can mail them back to you next week," I told the salesman.

One early afternoon the following week, I got a clear message from God's spirit which solved the housing problem. As I lectured I was drawing a transistor circuit on the blackboard. Just as clear as could be, God's spirit said to me, "Go to Elk Mound and buy your mobile home."

I was startled, but my students didn't seem to have heard anything. I finished the lecture, telephoned Patricia to get the boys ready, and told her we were going to Elk Mound to buy a mobile home. She only said, "Elk Mound? . . . Ok, I'll get them ready."

Elk Mound was a cross-roads community, with two stop signs, on the old road to Eau Claire. As we arrived, I saw on one of the four corners what looked like a Mom and Pop dealership for camping trailers. I decided that might be the place. Inside, an older gentleman was leaning back in an office chair. I asked him if he sold mobile homes.

"We sell camping trailers," he replied.

"No, I mean full-sized mobile homes to live in."

"I guess I could sell you one. I am an authorized dealer, but you would have to set it up yourself. I don't do that kind of work anymore."

I was relieved. "I know how to set one up if I can get it delivered to the lot."

"Where do you want it delivered?"

"Urbana, Illinois," I responded without batting an eye.

"I can do that and save you a lot by not having it delivered here," he replied.

The mobile home was the same unit listed in the Illinois dealer's sales contract. The Lord saved me $5,000 by purchasing in Wisconsin and agreeing to set up the unit myself. The savings represented purchasing at a 40% discount in 1969 dollars. But, of even greater significance to me was the apparent confirmation that I wasn't crazy in making the plans I was implementing for the future of my family. "If God be for us, who can be against us?" (Romans 8:31b).

Moving to Urbana, Illinois

Preparations for our move went smoothly. The new mobile home was to come furnished with furniture and appliances. When I had explored how much I could reduce the price by purchasing an unfurnished unit, I found the reduction to be a pittance. We were able to sell much of our household furniture and some appliances, accumulating enough funds, we thought, to see us through the summer so that Patricia would not have to get a job in a hurry. My temporary faculty replacement was currently serving a foreign assignment in Africa, but his friend gave us a security deposit on our home and assured us that the home was rented for the year. We loaded up the van and pulled a U-Haul with the remainder of our assets toward Urbana, Illinois.

When we arrived, the lot was empty! Telephone calls back to Wisconsin, and their calls to Indiana, indicated that the factory was behind a couple of weeks on production and delivery schedules. With time on our hands, we decided to take a short vacation through southern Canada and on to Fabius, New York.

Natural Gas Explosion Averted

When we returned to Urbana our home was setting on the lot ready for me to set it up properly. I purchased concrete blocks and commercial setup jacks to support the main floor. Telephone and electrical services were connected and started. The natural gas man came to mount the gas meter, connect the gas line, and turn it on. When he opened the main gas valve, there was an awful "whooshing" sound from within the mobile home. Immediately, both the gas man and I knew what the problem was, but we didn't want to believe it. He quickly shut off the gas, while I cleared my family out of the unit. We were only one spark away from an explosion. I carefully opened the windows to allow the prairie wind to clear out the gas that had escaped. Then we inspected the gas-using appliances. None of them were connected to the central gas supply line, and all supply line valves were wide open. There were no warning signs or labels to indicate the appliances were not ready for service.

The gas representative said, "Making these connections is not my responsibility, but I would have to come back again when you got these things ready. I'll help you connect them." God bless him! Together, we didn't take long to put all appliances into safe operation.

The Unseen Hand saves my doctorate program

Another very serious problem, almost fatal to the whole PhD program, developed due to my own naive misunderstanding of the meaning of "out-of-state tuition." In the University Catalog, I had noticed a big difference in tuition and fees between in-state and out-of-state residents. However, I hadn't worried because, in my mind, I was going to be a two-year resident of Illinois. I reasoned that if I had a residence, a postal address, a local banking account, and an Illinois driver's license, I must be a resident of Illinois. I carried documentation of all these proofs with me when I went to register and pay my summer school tuition and fees. I was expecting to pay approximately $370.

I was shocked when the clerk said, "That will be $3,700."

"What? Why?"

"How long have you lived in Illinois?"

"About a month," I replied, "but, I am a resident."

I attempted to show her my proof. She didn't even want to look at it.

"You moved to Illinois to go to school, so you are not a resident as far as the University of Illinois is concerned. Please pay, or move out of the way!"

I looked behind me. The waiting line had grown long. I looked in the back of the checkbook which my bookkeeper, Patricia, had entrusted me to carry for the day. There was a balance of just over $3,700 showing. I had been supremely confident that it was God's will for me to go to school. I had too much invested and no place to go if I backed out now. I shrugged my shoulders and wrote the check.

On the way home, I wondered how I could explain to Patricia that I had just blown all our expense money for the summer. ***Then it hit me!*** This was just the summer session. In September, the University would probably expect more than $5,000 for a full semester, then $5,000 more in January. Even if she found a job immediately, there was no way we would be able to afford to continue in the fall. I decided since I had already paid for the summer, I would complete those classes and seek a job myself in the fall. I beat myself up. How could I have been so naive not to understand the University's definition of the term, "resident"? Just as Peter had gone back to fishing, even after the resurrection and the appearances of Jesus (John 21:3), I was resigned to return to carpentry, at least long enough to get back to some professional job. I did not ask for, or anticipate, the wondrous solution the Lord was already preparing for me!

I returned home just ahead of lunch and faced Patricia with the bad news. There was not one word of rebuke, criticism, or questioning of my intelligence or judgment. She said, "After lunch, you watch the boys, and I will go look for a job."

It was Friday afternoon. I put the Chip and Rick down for a nap and went to check the status of our food supplies. Like *Old Mother Hubbard*, the cupboards were bare. The refrigerator had a little milk, ketchup, and other condiments. I was in despair. Even if we had a credit card at the time (which we didn't), grocery stores were not allowed to accept them. I knelt down in front of the sofa and started to pray. "Lord, what am I going to do? I don't understand. Why I am in this mess? I thought I was following your guidance . . ." As I was praying, the new phone rang.

"Who even knows our number?" I thought as I answered it. The caller was my new Department Head.

"I have checked your record; you supervised student teachers back at Montclair, didn't you?"

"Yes,"

"Would you like to supervise student teachers for us?" he asked.

WOULD I? YOU BET! He went on to explain that the graduate fellow who was scheduled to supervise had suddenly resigned to go to Israel. He was offering me a half-time fellowship to fill that position. The fellowship paid a salary and all fees and tuition, even for out-of-state residents. The fellow had also walked out on a half-time grant for summer research work which I could take over immediately if that was my desire.

OF COURSE IT WAS MY DESIRE!

"By the way," he said, "if you can get down here this afternoon, I will have the paper work ready for you to take to the Business Office and pick up a refund of your charges."

"Patricia has the van," I said, "As soon as she comes home, I will be there."

Then my prayer changed. Aloud, I cried, "Thank you God! Please send Patricia home so that I can get this taken care of before the Office closes."

Chip had sensed the excitement and gotten up. I didn't even try to put him back to bed. We were about eight miles from the Department Head's office, and another three miles back to the Business Office, so there was no possibility of walking.

Patricia had searched for a job and finally decided to come back home in defeat for the day. It was about four-thirty when she drove in. Normally, we always take the time to explain our actions to each other. That makes for a smoother marriage, but there was no time for explanations now. I opened her van door with one hand and hauled her out with the other saying, "Everything is OK. I'll explain later!"

I left her bewildered, made the circuit to the Department Head's office, signed the papers he had prepared, and arrived at the Business Office window just as it was closing. The clerk stopped her action and took my papers.

"Do you want a check or cash?" She asked.

As no banks were open late on Friday evenings back then, I hopefully said, "Cash."

She counted out $3,700 into my hand! We were able to celebrate by going grocery shopping that evening.

In retrospect, if I had understood the University's definition of "residents," I would not have had the faith or courage to make the move which jeopardized the family's welfare at the time that I did. If in the planning stages I had applied for a fellowship, I would have been told that there was a long waiting line for openings in the future. I would not have been where I needed to be when the opportunity arose! Sometimes, the Unseen Hand uses innocent ignorance and blind faith to work out God's purpose.

My PhD. Studies Begin

I was assigned a Graduate Advisor to help me plan my doctorate program. The Catalog specified 60 semester hours of "Approved Course Work" and a dissertation. There was a planning sheet showing required courses and blanks for options and electives. I asked if the courses I had completed the summer before during the National Science Foundation Institute could count.

"Yes, they count," my advisor replied. "See, I have them listed right over here under the elective list."

"Then I don't really need a full 60 hours of course work, do I?" I asked.

"Oh yes you do," he answered. "Those courses were taken before you were admitted to the program."

I decided not to push the lack of logic I sensed here. Since I had refused to take a foreign language in high school, I opted to use computer languages to meet the special language requirement. Fortunately, this was a new option in their PhD program. I still was not interested in administration, so I elected to take my minor field in Educational Research and Statistics.

In addition to the required courses on the history and philosophy of education and common research methods, I was pleased to take a computer orientation course which would enable me to submit programs to the mainframe computer. They taught us how to use the card punching machine, gave us account charging codes, and taught us how to use the California Bio-Med program package to do statistical analysis of data. My fellowship account (which I didn't have to pay) was charged each time I submitted a program by the amount of time the computer spent on the problem, measured in milliseconds, and the amount of paper used in the printout report.

Students still couldn't actually see or touch the computer. We submitted our card stack at an acceptance window. The cards were read and the data stored in the order received on a batch tape waiting to be mounted on the computer. We usually got our cards back in five minutes. Then, two hours or more might pass before the tape with our program was mounted and ran. The printed reports were picked up at the "OUTPUT WINDOWS." These twenty-six windows were ordered alphabetically to help us find our printouts by our last names. Any little mistake on any one card resulted in a printout with the word "FLUSHED" in a big image across the front. Getting a non-flushed print was a challenge for beginners. I was in awe of the people I saw carrying long trays of over 1,000 cards each. The computer center ran twenty-four hours a day, seven days a week, with no holidays. I soon learned that submitting cards in the wee hours of the morning resulted in a faster turn-around of results. Patricia was much faster than I on the keyboard, so too often I imposed on her to bring the boys and key punch my program from the sheets I had prepared. We took a foam pad with us for the boys to play and sleep on as we worked.

In early fall, Patricia got a full-time job with health benefits as a secretary/bookkeeper for a local manufacturer of concrete block and pipe. The company was very good to her, and she was able to remain in their employ until I completed the program and we moved to Virginia.

Chip started first grade in the University Demonstration School, and Richard was placed in a church-related daycare program near Chip's school. My work for the fellowship, visiting student teachers in local schools, was very flexible; and most of my classes were in the evening, so I was generally free to be the family's taxi driver, delivering and picking up family members. Eventually, I was able to find a well-used Volkswagen Beetle, and for the first time, we became a two car family.

A church home in Illinois

With our work, school and home issues settled, we still needed to find a church family. We became acquainted with some of the friendly workers at the charismatic church which sponsored Richard's day care and visited there. Their worship style was a relatively new experience for us, but these people loved the Lord and were free from the questionable practices we had heard associated with some Pentecostal movements. They prayed for the sick, but never claimed that illnesses were caused by the patient's sin, or that the failure to observe a miraculous healing was a result of weak faith. They gathered an offering, but never claimed that the gift was a "seed" that would grow into multiple blessings from the Lord. Nobody was "slain" in the Spirit. The congregation was a mixture of middle class workers, a few farmers, some military couples from Rantoul Air Force Base, and fellow graduate student couples. The pastor was a calm, but thorough expositor of biblical truths and the special vocabulary born again Christians use to describe their spiritual experiences. He exhibited the gift of interpretation. Only occasionally would someone be moved to speak in tongues, and then the pastor would interpret. Usually the message was encouraging us to recognize God, trust Him, and worship with a clean heart. One time, however, a stranger was in the congregation and started speaking words we did not understand. The pastor stopped him sharply.

"You are speaking the most blasphemous words one can say in the language you are using. You are not to say another word." The man was silent the rest of the service, and we never saw him again.

We also found ways to use our particular gifts. Patricia played the piano while the pastor's wife played the organ. I was eventually convinced to teach a senior citizens' class. I also helped the pastor with calling on visitors. We started up a couples' club which grew by leaps and bounds, providing good fun and fellowship. Once a month our whole family ministered to a nursing home. The older ladies really enjoyed seeing Chip and Richard. I also helped do the wiring for the parsonage that the church was building through volunteer labor.

PhD program saved again

During the fall and spring semesters of 1969-70, I thought I had made real progress on the completion of the required courses and my minor field. At the end of the spring semester, I had a progress evaluation meeting with my Advisor. He seemed pleased with my work to date, but indicated I still had major weaknesses that I should make up by extra course work. I asked him what I needed to do to complete the program.

"Sixty hours of approved course work and a dissertation."

"But that is what I needed when I started," I protested.

He gave me a lame excuse that "approved course work" was selected to fill in weaknesses in my background. He said that he used his professional judgment in individual cases, and that I would still need sixty hours plus a dissertation.

"But, you have approved everything I have scheduled," I said. "And I have passed everything with good grades."

He repeated his contention, "My job is to make such judgments."

The more I thought about the situation, the more I felt as if I had been spinning my wheels. This was before the days when students learned that they had legal rights. We didn't evaluate our professors or their courses as is the practice today. A professor's word was assumed to be next to law! I could not go back to Stout at this point because they had already hired a substitute for me for the coming year. I felt I had to try to chart another course. I checked the job openings in our professional journals and discovered that Eastern Illinois University needed a technology professor for the coming academic year. The University was close enough so that I could commute. If I could get an appointment to that position, Patricia could keep her job, and we would not have to move the family. Maybe I could continue to take evening classes.

I took my resume and visited the Eastern Illinois University Department Head. The interview went well. When I returned home, my own Department Head called me.

"What is going on?" he demanded. "I just got a call from Eastern Illinois University wanting a recommendation for you for their position."

I explained what had happened at my last meeting with my advisor. I had spent a year and was no closer to my degree than when I started.

"You come to see me tomorrow morning, and we will straighten this out," he said.

"What about my Advisor?"

"Don't worry about him. I am now your Advisor." he replied.

At my conference with my new Advisor, he reviewed my record, gave me credit for everything I had taken, and assured me that I was on track to finish my course work and do the dissertation during the coming year. He said he had wondered why some other apparently promising students had suddenly quit the program after their first year. I have learned since that some of my professional friends had similar experiences in other graduate schools. Apparently, some advisors want to hang on to their existing students for fear that no new students will enroll. I never saw my old advisor again. It was rumored among the graduate students that he suddenly left the University of Illinois for a position somewhere in the Carolinas. Again, "All things work together for good . . ."

Like Paul on Mars Hill

Student attendees of our church were active in campus groups affiliated with such national organizations as Youth for Christ and Intervarsity Christian Fellowship. The ministry of Josh McDowell of Campus Crusade for Christ International was well known for lecturing about and debating the truths of the scripture. Some students in these groups at the University of Illinois envisioned a ministry event something like a Josh McDowell visit that would present the gospel in a challenging way. They planned to bring Arthur Katz, a bold proponent of the faith, on campus for a special ministry. At this point in his career, Arthur Katz was presenting the Gospel and contending strongly for the faith against those who held his former Marxist/atheist positions. Quoting from a web site:

> Arthur "Art" Katz (February 13, 1929-June 28, 2007) was an author and Christian preacher who traveled the world teaching an alternative to what he described as today's "make nice" Christianity. Born to Jewish parents, he was a self-proclaimed Marxist/atheist who was converted to Christianity while taking a year sabbatical from his Oakland, California, teaching job and traveling through Europe in 1963. (http://en.wikipedia.org/wiki/Arthur_Katz)

Being busy with my own studies, I first became aware of something special happening when I saw big posters with the message, "HE IS COMING!" on poles and bulletin boards around campus. "Who is coming?" I wondered. A week later, the posters were changed to read, "ARTHUR KATZ IS COMING!" "Who is he?" I wondered again. Then at a prayer service in church, we were asked to pray for the success of the meetings with Arthur Katz. We were given a brief summary of his background and methods. He was to arrive at the Student Union at noon the next day and make his first presentation.

Normally, I did not go to the Student Union, but I took my lunch and went that day. The big dining room had tables scattered around with food services and vending areas on the perimeter. There was the usual clinking of dishes, drinking glasses, and silverware with a background of conversational hum as maybe 200 students were getting food and eating. I sat at an empty table in the corner to eat my lunch and observe what might happen.

From a side entrance, a tall, dark-haired man with sharp eyes appeared. He started introducing himself in an authoritative voice, projecting in volume a little above conversational level. Only a few people seemed to hesitate in their activities to take notice of him. He gave his testimony as a former Marxist, atheist Jew who had studied the scriptures and found a new life and faith in the teachings of Jesus Christ. He simply presented the "Good News" of the gospel, as an exposition of John 3:16: That God loved us all enough to send His Son, Jesus, to take the punishment for our sins. Those who believed were promised freedom from guilt through the forgiveness of personal sin and eternal life in heaven. He explained that no other system of beliefs promised followers that much.

Arthur Katz talked for fifteen minutes at most with no visible reaction from the audience.

Then he said, "I am issuing an invitation to any one of you to believe these truths in your own heart. If you want to change your spiritual life, repeat after me the Sinner's Prayer, but, only do this if you really mean it."

He bowed his head, and the room went silent. I mean really silent! Many people had been listening after all.

"Lord, I know that I am a sinner." he started and waited.

Then a voice was heard from the middle of the room. "Lord, I am a sinner," and then another, and a third one.

Katz led them through acknowledging Christ as their savior, asking for forgiveness and help to live a life pleasing to God. When Katz and the followers finished, slowly the hum and tinkle of the crowd came back to normal. I wondered if the Apostle Paul, when he preached to the Greeks on Mars Hill, felt the same satisfaction after he finished as I did that day. And I was not the preacher!

Arthur Katz also preached a couple of times in our church while he was in the area. Being raised as a Jew, he was able to shed meaningful light on such Jewish celebrations as the Passover and Hanukah. I did not realize that even today, Jewish families spent a week physically and ritually scouring their house of anything unclean before the celebration of the Passover. The number of college students attending our services increased greatly as a result of the lectures and debates he participated in on campus.

Experiencing student protests

The winter and spring of 1970 saw a great increase in the strength of emotions and the number of active protests among students against the Vietnam War. Many of the protesters went beyond legal rights of assembly and protest into civil disobedience, endangering others who had no control over political policy or the war. In Urbana, a public school bus was turned on its side blocking the main campus street. Also, the University Administration Building was blocked. A curfew was imposed. We started driving the boys to and from school for their own safety. If possible, we avoided travel near the center of campus. There, and in many places around the country, the National Guard was used to help keep order. However, at first the various state governments forbid the guards to keep live ammunition in their weapons. Believing they were in no real danger, some students went beyond human decency in their interactions with the Guard. There were rumors of such things as filling balloons with urine before throwing the balloons in the faces of the guards. On May 4, 1970, mistrust, lack of real control, and bad relations culminated in the Ohio National Guard being armed and firing on students at Kent State University. Some among the injured and dead were reported to be totally innocent. News of the event spread across the country and had a sobering effect on all involved. There were limits to, and consequences for, irresponsible behavior after all. A high price had been paid to learn that lesson. In the region of the University of Illinois, more responsible behavior was followed by the community feeling safer.

Qualifying exams

The culmination of all doctoral studies is the passing of major and supporting field examinations and the defense of a dissertation. In my case, there were separate examinations on the history and philosophy of my major field, the application of advanced statistics to experimental research models, the application of computers to research and educational problems, and on proficiency in using computer languages. There were days of testing! I passed everything on the first try except the exam in my major field. That was a surprise!

My advisor assured me that failing the major field exam the first time was not an unusual experience. Failing anything was unusual for me! He said that one of my professors thought that my responses were too "parochial." My responses to the questions indicated too much commitment to industrial arts as general education at the neglect of the broad range of vocational education programs. As far as commitment was concerned, he was right. Foolish me, I thought the test was to measure my knowledge, not my commitment.

By keeping my ears open, I learned that the professor's real problem was political. One of the questions asked why there was no federal funding for industrial arts programs. I had explained that the Congress writing the current vocational education act had considered industrial arts to be part of general education. Since the Constitution of the United States does not even mention education, then all general education was considered a state responsibility. The federal government only supported special programs by specific acts of Congress. The professor thought I should have made strong arguments for the new liberal position that the federal government should be supporting all of education. I am a fast learner. Knowing that at least one faculty member expected me to respond way beyond the bounds of any question asked, and that he wanted me to support his political advocacy, I passed my major field test on the second try.

Dissertation research

For my dissertation, I decided to study the relationship between male students' maturation during adolescent development and their perceptual motor skills that would be important in training for skilled trades. Current practice was to place all adolescent junior high boys into beginning woodworking regardless of physical development. They were given the same hand tools that adults would be using on a job. They were assigned projects using the tools and graded on their success. Some, like me, had thrived with this opportunity. However, I had observed that many floundered, lacking strength, coordination, steady hands, or some combination of perceptual motor development to perform as expected. Studies had also shown that many males who had a bad school shop experience misjudged their abilities after they had matured. I thought if we could easily identify boys not mature enough to succeed through no fault of their own, we could possibly provide a better educational program with more realistic goals for them. My research did support concerns that the current curriculum was not suited to the maturity levels of some adolescent males.

As I went into the summer of 1971, finishing the dissertation and getting a fall teaching position became priorities. I could go back to Stout, but they could not offer me much of a raise because the State of Wisconsin was cutting budgets; and I was already on their pay schedule. In the Department Head's files I found an announcement of a position in vocational-industrial teacher education at Virginia Polytechnic Institute (VPI), Blacksburg, Virginia. I applied, underwent the interview process, and soon had a contract doubling the salary I had left at Stout.

As we worked to complete the dissertation, the generation of error free progress reports and final drafts, without modern word-processing, was tedious. Each section of the report had to be hand written, submitted to Patricia for typing, and then submitted to the faculty committee members for their review and suggestions. Often, their suggestions became demands in conflict with another member's suggestions. I had to resolve differences to everybody's satisfaction. Then the final draft chapters of the dissertation were prepared. Library standards of the University demanded perfect typing. No erasures were allowed. One misspelling or typographical error resulted in the whole page being retyped.

We had to move to Blacksburg, Virginia, before the dissertation was complete. Both Patricia and I were burned out! In the late fall, when all committee members were satisfied, we sent what we thought was the final copy to Illinois. We heaved a sigh of relief, but our patience was really tested when the Committee Chair called with bad news. The final draft was basically fine with everybody—except for one major detail. Since each chapter represented a final report in an on-going process, they were written largely in the present tense. Everything, except recommendations for future research, had to be translated into the past tense. To make matters worse, there was an impending date for acceptance to be met in order for me to be cleared for the winter graduation. If I didn't graduate then, I would have to modify my contract with VPI. The document was over 100 pages long!

Patricia was understandably frustrated. "I have already typed this thing four times. If I type it again this time, we have no guarantee that they will not come up with some other reason to reject it."

She was right, of course. She was also right in expressing the feeling that I, or at least one of the Committee members, should have been aware of the requirement before the final draft; but, as it had always been with us, failure was not an option! We pulled together and placed the final draft in Express Delivery just in time for the Committee Chair to hand walk it through the administrative channels, clearing me for graduation.

At graduation time, I was so financially strapped and mentally fatigued from finishing the dissertation while keeping up with my new duties at VPI that I didn't even consider traveling back to Illinois for the ceremony. I realized later that this was a selfish decision on my part. After all of Patricia's hard work and sacrifices in so many ways, she would have felt proud and fulfilled to see me walk the aisle.

CHAPTER 16

LIVING AND TEACHING IN VIRGINIA

The move to Blacksburg

The move to our new home in Blacksburg, Virginia, had its own unlikely events. We had sold the house in Wisconsin to help with living expenses during graduate studies. I was initially considering the possibility of moving our mobile home. When we made a trip to Virginia to explore housing possibilities, I discovered there was no financial advantage in moving the unit rather than selling it and renting or purchasing something else in Blacksburg.

In 1971, Blacksburg was a small university town with just enough businesses to serve students and faculty. Housing was tighter than it had been in Menomonie. The limited rental property there was tied up in leases, mostly to married students, and very few new housing subdivisions were under construction. During our search for housing, the salesman for one of the local builders showed us a new, three-bedroom brick home under construction and referred us to a local bank. The bank representative was incredulous that we would try to purchase real estate without the traditional down payment. Nevertheless, in comparing the price the builder was willing to accept against the assessed value of the home, and after checking our excellent credit rating, he reluctantly indicated that he could arrange special financing for a VPI University professor, making it possible for us to purchase the home. Among other decisions regarding the completion of the house, Patricia was able choose her carpet and paint colors. The building was to be complete by the time we needed it for the fall semester. Our mobile home in Illinois sold almost immediately after we advertised it.

Patricia enrolled the boys in the school system which was growing so fast that facilities had not kept up with the need. Chip's class was in what had been, before integration, a one-room school house for black children. Richard's class was in a church with heavy curtains separating class groups. New facilities were only in the planning stages. We were surprised that a university community was that far behind.

Teaching at VPI

In my new position at Virginia Polytechnic Institute (VPI), I was the junior member of the faculty team to deliver VPI's instructional services to the new area vocational schools and community colleges scattered around Virginia. Concurrently, we were operating a Bachelor of Science Degree program in Vocational-Industrial Education on campus. We had no local shops because our teachers and BS degree candidates were expected to already have at least two years of employment in their trade or occupation. As degreed teacher trainers, we also had to have 2,000 hours of employment in a trade or occupation. That is why my having to postpone college to work right after high school became critically important in the overall plan of my life. I was easily able to document my trade experiences. We taught professional education courses such as teaching methods, occupational analysis, curriculum development, laboratory safety, and use of audio-visual aids. These courses were based on generic principles that could be applied by any teacher regardless of the specific occupational training he or she was conducting.

The vocational-industrial instructor preparation model represented a major shifting of instructional challenges for me. In industrial arts programs, I taught knowledge and skills which might be useful as a hobby or in any general situation in life. Now, the vocational instructors

I was preparing were charged with specific training for a specific trade or occupation. Because most of my student instructors did not have BS degrees, I tried to advise them on an academic path to the degree. In a particular field class, such as teaching methods, I was supposed to critique a practicing hair dresser as she taught a lesson on hair coloring, followed by a mason's lesson on safely cutting bricks, and then an auto mechanic's demonstration on how to change the oil in a car, or a nurse's instruction using a fever thermometer. Of course, each instructor was confident that I knew nothing about his or her specialty. I had to use all of Dale Carnegie's principles of human relations to make corrections and suggestions that would be accepted by them and help them in their teaching. By reinforcing good performance elements, overlooking nit-picky faults, and making positive alternative suggestions, I won their confidence.

Unfortunately, I was teaching field classes on the road too much of the time. The senior faculty team member had scheduled the classes the previous year. I might have a class in Winchester, Virginia, a five-hour drive northeast, on Tuesday and a class in Abington, three hours southwest, on Thursday. In order to justify the three hours of college credit that could be earned, classes were three hours long. VPI reimbursed travel expenses with meals and lodging if I decided to spend the night. I could fly from Roanoke to Washington, DC, for classes in that area if I desired, but the scheduled return flight was so late that I could drive to my home quicker. I had a family that I wanted to see, so I usually drove home the same day, getting there in the middle of the night. The Department Chair promised me that after two years in the field, I would be assigned full time at the campus.

When the rest of the faculty in the Vocational-Technical Education Department realized my statistical background, I was asked to serve on faculty committees reviewing Master's degree theses and oral exams. One semester, The School of Education assigned me to teach the masters level Introduction to Educational Research and Statistics course to elementary teachers.

Lee R. Clendenning, PhD

Seeing the Sights in Virginia

In addition to my solo teaching travels all over the state, sometimes schedules could be timed right to take Patricia and the boys along on exploratory trips. Virginia is a beautiful state. The Blue Ridge Parkway was especially pretty in the fall as the leaves changed. The Shenandoah Valley provided good scenery regardless of season. I taught enough in the Washington, DC, area to eventually visit all the memorials and the Smithsonian Institution as well as Mount Vernon and the Capital Buildings. The boys may have been too young to remember much of these travels or the real significance of what they were seeing, but for a country boy like me, who had not aspired to get very far out of central New York at their age, the experiences were very impressive.

Looking for a church home again

We never found a real church home in Blacksburg. How much of that was our fault is difficult to evaluate. There were more cultural differences between local Blacksburg residents and those in other places we had lived. We were reminded that Virginia was the heart of the Confederacy. Virginia also had a long history of tobacco growing and use. The link between smoking and cancer was still being ignored or denied in many circles. Even though I knew in my head that God loved these people, smoke and all, it was still unsettling to have to walk through the smokers on the church steps to get into a service.

The second year, we tried a Southern Baptist Church, our first experience with that denomination. The church had a sizeable contingent of college students and seemed to be growing. The pastor preached a series of sermons on the ordinance of baptism. He and I agreed that there was no promise of salvation in the ordinance. However, he brought to my attention that a person should be baptized after commitment of his or her life to Christ as a testimony of faith to the rest of the world. Thinking about my meaningless dunking with the family at the age of eight, I decided that I needed to be baptized again now that it would be meaningful. The pastor very willingly accommodated me.

The decision to leave Virginia

In the late spring of 1973, events occurred which resulted in our leaving Virginia. First, the Department Chair, who had promised me that I would only have to travel the roads for VPI for two years, unexpectedly retired. The new Department Chair scheduled me for mostly road work for the coming 1973-74 academic year. When questioned about the situation, he said that he needed the more mature faculty (such as me) to deal with the older students in the field. I suppose I should have been flattered. He had gotten approval to offer graduate assistanceships to master's degree candidates to help with the on-campus undergraduates. In fact, he wanted the industrial-vocational team to recruit some outstanding candidates for these positions.

To implement a national search for graduate assistants, my colleague and I divided the *National Directory of Vocational-Technical Teacher Education Programs* between us. By chance (my thinking at the time), I took the listings from A to L while my colleague took the rest. We were to call the departmental office of each program listed to make department heads aware of the new opportunity at VPI and to discuss any possible candidates they might suggest.

When I called Berry College, the Department Head was not available, so I talked with the Dean of the College. We developed a friendly rapport almost immediately. After I presented VPI's opportunity, the Dean started asking more personal and professional questions about me. How did an obvious Yankee wind up in a southern university? What did I teach? What did I really like to teach? What had I taught in other places? I thought the questions were a little probing, but maybe he was just going overboard to be friendly. Cutting him short would not serve my purpose in calling him. Before the conversation ended, he told me a little bit about Berry College.

My colleague was able to identify good candidates during his calls, and the positions on campus were filled.

The second event prompting a move was another accident. Our Southern Baptist Church had decided to construct an additional building for Sunday school rooms. A volunteer work day was called to cut trees off the lot in preparation for the foundation. I was sure that there was no better woodsman in the church than me. I still had my good chopping axe from the farm. When I reported for work, the volunteers had only one chain saw. I told the apparent foreman that if they used the chain saw to cut the trees off the stump and the limbs away from the trunk, I would be happy to trim and cut the branches into firewood lengths. A fellow volunteer, one of my college students, was to assist me. I set up a heavy wood block to chop against. My student was to place long limbs over the block for me to cut off and then to advance the limb about eighteen inches for the next cut.

The system was working fine for the first hour. The small crew was impressed. They had never seen what a good ax man could do with a sharp blade. Most cuts only took one swing, and we were keeping up with the chainsaw crew. The only problem was one of safety. I had instructed my helper to make sure the spot to be cut was laid flat against the block to prevent the cut off end from flying. In fairness, he had never seen a limb fly, so he was repeatedly careless about how he held the limb. After I had refused to swing until he repositioned the limb a few times, he again pushed the limb forward with one end slightly high. I thought, "It isn't off by much, it's not worth correcting him again." I swung the ax. Blink, and the lights went out! The cut off end of the limb had flipped in the air and hit my nose from the right side, breaking the bones and cartilage into seven pieces and pushing most of my nose to the left under my eye. When I came to, some volunteers took me to the local hospital; in those days there was no 911 service. Personnel monitoring Blacksburg's small hospital didn't know what to do with me, so they sent me home!

Patricia cleaned me up and called a friend who had been in the area for years. This friend contacted her personal physician who arranged for us to meet with a nasal specialist on an emergency basis in Roanoke, fifty miles away. The specialist was recently discharged from military service in Vietnam, and said he had set a dozen to fifteen noses a day over there. He explained that if the stick had hit me an inch closer to my face it would have sent bones into my brain and killed me, an inch further away and it would have missed me. He thought I was lucky. That day, the doctor tried to reset most of the bones and cartilage. After I had passed out from the pain three times, he said I would have to return on

Monday morning to their specialty hospital where he would finish the job under anesthesia. I missed classes for the rest of the week.

No member of the church, not even the pastor, came to visit me, called to check on my condition, or offered to help in any way. A new professor and his wife had been visiting the church as we were doing. They dropped off a chocolate cake. He told us the congregants were afraid to make contact with us because they were worried that anything they might say could be used against the church in a lawsuit. He brought us further disappointing news: The church had cancelled any further volunteer work days.

During the week of my recovery, I had time to take stock of my life in general. I wasn't seeing the boys much because I had to leave for classes before they came home from school, and they were asleep by the time I returned home in the early morning. Many mornings I didn't get up in time to see them at breakfast. I told Patricia that if this continued, one day I would be getting an invitation to their graduation without really knowing them. VPI had provided a grand learning experience for me. My professional resume and real instructional experiences had moved way beyond industrial arts crafts and technical electronics. Blacksburg and the mountain environment provided a wonderful place to live. Nevertheless, it was clear that over the long term I was going to have to find a different position. Again, like Mary, the mother of Jesus, I started pondering these things in my heart.

I had read or heard somewhere that the first law of wing-walking was: "Keep a firm hold where you are as you reach for the next handhold." I was reluctant to start a formal search for a new position, knowing that such a move might burn bridges behind me in my current position. When I saw an announcement for a position at Berry College, I quietly applied without notice to VPI. I was almost through the summer assignments without realizing that the "Unseen Hand" was working on a solution to my personal and professional problems.

As I was conducting the last class meeting of the term in a rented meeting room at Dulles International Airport, I was interrupted by a facility representative saying I had a long distance call from Georgia. As I went to take the call, I wondered how anybody knew where to contact me. Patricia and the boys were waiting for me at a nearby motel, but even she did not have a number to reach me. The call was from the Dean of Berry College. The Dean asked if I remembered our previous conversation.

"Yes, I do," I answered.

The Dean explained that he had reviewed my academic record and professional work. He was sure that I was the right person for a position they had in the Industrial Education Department at Berry College.

"I know you are the kind of person who would be challenged by the mission we serve. We are trying to provide a good education to students with little financial means, but who are willing to work. Our current Department Head must retire in one year. We are looking for someone like you to pick up the Department leadership after a year's orientation. We just renovated the industrial education facilities. We really need help in the professional education sequence, electronics and graphic arts. Will you come to Berry and see what we have, and see how you would fit into our mission? We will reimburse your travel expenses."

He hesitated in his obvious sales pitch. I had twice noticed the word "mission," but I was somewhat dumbfounded. Stalling for time to gather my wits, I said, "If I come for an interview, I would need to bring my wife and family."

I will never forget the Dean's immediate response. "If you don't bring your family, there is no point in your coming. We are completely family orientated here."

He had me on the hook. The Dean and I quickly made an appointment for meeting on the following Sunday afternoon, with the formal interviews to follow on Monday.

Chapter 17

The Move to Georgia— Berry College

Visiting Berry College

Patricia and I had to cancel one last Washington, DC, sightseeing tour. During the morning following the Dean's call, we returned to Blacksburg and started packing for an exploratory trip to Georgia. Patricia was less than excited about this possible move. For the first time in our marriage, she was finally in a real, modern home, with a true friend in another faculty member's wife. She loved the mountains. In many respects, Georgia felt like a foreign assignment to her; yet she did not drag her heels.

In 1973, the trip from Blacksburg, Virginia, to Rome, Georgia, was tiring. Interstates south of the Virginia/Tennessee border were only completed in short sections. It was two lane road most of the way. We were tired as we arrived at Berry College early in the afternoon. Our idea was to snoop around incognito before our meeting with the Dean.

I stopped by the posted campus map at the Security Gate House. We could look through the gate and see the apparent and impressive main administrative building, Hermann Hall. As I was getting out of the car to inspect the map, someone parked his car just ahead of us, got out, and called, "You are looking for the Waterwheel. Follow me and I will take you there!" He then started ahead slowly.

"Waterwheel?" I thought, "I didn't know there was a waterwheel." I have always been intrigued by windmills and water wheels, so I started following my volunteer guide. We went past the entrance circle, Hermann Hall, and a scenic lake, and then headed for what I now know to be the Mountain Campus. We didn't know there would be three miles of wilderness. Patricia glanced at me as if my driveway did not go all the way to my garage.

"We planned to explore, didn't we?" I offered.

The mountain campus had neatly mown lawns and well-maintained natural stone buildings. But, of course, we did not know what we were seeing. We threaded our way around to the back side of the campus and started into the woods on a graveled road. Then I had a sudden feeling that I was going home. I grew up on such a road, except we had patches of grass between tire-worn strips. I didn't know what Patricia was thinking. She likes civilization. We soon came into a clearing in the woods. My guide stopped ahead and pointed right. I crossed a stone culvert over a stream before stopping. On my right I saw the tallest waterwheel in the world, 42 feet tall, turning slowly. I exited the car and gazed with my mouth agape. My guide was gone with a wave of his hand. I have always wondered who he was.

Revealing the Unseen Hand

Patricia and I at Berry's Water Wheel, 2012

The rest of the family left the car to stretch their legs and explore. I wondered how the water was forced to the top of the wheel because there was not a traditional spillway or pump, just a tall column behind the wheel. Also unique was a big ring gear all the way around the outside. This gear drove a small pinion follower gear mounted on a shaft. A clutch lever engaged or disengaged the rotation of the pinion shaft into the millhouse. The boys threw stones in the water. Later, Patricia told friends that when she saw the wheel, she knew she was "done for." She reportedly thought, "If they offer him a job as a janitor, he'll take it."

We returned to the main campus, drove around the Ford Buildings, toured what was obviously "Faculty Row," and then continued into the city of Rome. Federal Route 27 became Second Avenue which went over a river through a high bridge with steel superstructure before crossing the main "Broad Street." The downtown section of Rome reminded me of small cities in upstate New York. There were older buildings, department stores, "Five and Dime" stores, and what appeared to be small restaurants. There were traffic lights at intersections and parking meters lined the sidewalks. We returned to campus to keep our appointment with the Dean.

The Dean and his wife were very gracious hosts. We were taken to a log cabin guest house and given time to unload and refresh before an official campus tour. They were proud of Berry's size (over 30,000 acres at the time), historical traditions, and traditional mission. We intellectually absorbed as much of it as we could in a hurry. There was a bon voyage party planned for an older, retired staff couple that evening which the Dean insisted we attend in order to meet new people. I later learned that the Dean neglected to tell the party hostess that we would be coming. It was a hot August evening, so the Dean arranged for Chip and Richard to swim in the pool associated with Memorial Gym. At the party, we did meet many older staff and alumni. Afterwards, I told Patricia that the Institution must have something positive going for it if people that old came back to socialize. There was no air conditioning in the guest log cabin assigned to us, so we spent a sweaty night.

On Monday, my official interviews began with a tour of the new Industrial Education facilities in the Laughlin Building. There were separate, well-equipped laboratories for drafting, woodworking, foundry, welding, electronics, photography, and machine shop with sheet metal. A large, mostly empty, area had been reserved for development of a program in graphic arts/printing. Conversation as we toured indicated that the Department also delivered elective courses for students in other programs such as agriculture, forestry, and communications, as well as architectural planning and drafting for home economics students interested in home planning. Then we toured the Jones Building, which housed the campus physical plant maintenance functions. Here were more shops with student workers supervised by mature tradesman in each area. Students learned the trades while working a paid schedule of twenty hours per week. Work hours were scheduled around their academic programs.

Graduates of the Industrial Education Department could prepare themselves for one of four career paths:

(1) Traditional industrial arts teaching in public schools.
(2) Teaching a vocational trade in the new secondary or post-secondary area vocational schools. (Student training in the physical plant would count toward the required 2,000 hours of employment.)
(3) Employment in private industry as operators, tradesmen, foremen, or managers of workers or operations. (These students often minored in Business Management.)
(4) Personal economic ventures to operate their own custom job shops, contracting business, or service.

I was deeply impressed with the facilities, the breadth of education provided, and the way practical work was organized to support the financial and educational needs of the students. I could see that being an effective administrator in this system would use all of the formal schooling and practical work experience I had ever acquired to that point in my career. The mission of providing a practical college education for those students willing to work was personally appealing. Room, board, and tuition were very low and could be covered over a four—year period with campus labor. I personally could have used such a program in my youth if I had known it existed. I also liked the idea of returning to practical, hands-on laboratory instruction.

We ate lunch in the old Blackstone Dining Hall, now the Young Theater, before proceeding to Oak Hill and the Martha Berry Museum where Inez Henry was the Director and our host. Inez showed us the locally produced film, *Miracle in the Mountains*, which depicted the life of Martha Berry as she founded and nurtured the Berry Schools from a Sunday school class to a coeducational college. By the time the film was finished, I was committed. Inez Henry had been a personal secretary to Martha Berry, and she kept us entertained by stories of how rich benefactors such as Henry Ford and William Randolph Hurst had been convinced to support the schools. Chip had developed an interest in history at a young age; he would ask a question, and she was off on another story. When we reminded her that we were already late for our appointment with the President, she bluntly said, "The President will wait until I am finished here." I thought, "OK?" I did not know at that time that she was also a long-time College Trustee.

President John Bertrand insisted that Patricia and the boys join us during my interview. The Dean also attended. The President spent more time talking with Chip and Richard than me. They were very polite and articulate. I don't know what he had already been told about us, but he did ask us if we could support the inter-denominational Christian mission of the institution. Of course, we could! The Dean presented a tentative employment package for me which the President approved on the spot. They offered me a step in academic rank to Associate Professor, a year of probation before assuming the role of Department Head, and a twelve-month contract at a salary matching what I was earning at VPI. I could rent Berry housing, and we were to quickly move to Georgia.

Moving again

Rather than face another Georgia night without air conditioning, we left the Guest Cabin late Monday afternoon and spent the night in Chattanooga. There, we gathered our wits regarding the hasty decision

I had made and what needed to be done in the immediate future. Even though Patricia was not enthusiastic about moving to Georgia, like the organizer she is, she composed an advertisement to sell our Virginia home. In the morning, she called in the advertisement to the newspaper in Christiansburg, Virginia. We spent the rest of the week untangling me from VPI and packing.

In her Sunday school class on the following Sunday, Patricia asked for prayer to help us find a buyer for our house. After the morning church service, she was approached by a stranger asking about the house, wanting to inspect it that afternoon. Patricia tried to put him off to a later date, saying that the house was definitely not ready for inspection, but, he was persistent. He said he was the new head football coach for VPI, and he had to find housing for his staff. They set a meeting time in the afternoon. Following his inspection, with no quibbling about the price we were asking, the coach laid a retainer check on the kitchen table. At the closing of the sale, we were able to pay off our mortgage for the house in Virginia.

In short order, I had rented a big U-Haul van, and managed to overdo while lifting and carrying, hurting my weak back afresh. Patricia's parents flew from New York to help us load the van and drive our second car to Georgia.

Berry housing

Berry assigned us to a house in Summerville Park, a residential area on the north side of Rome, next to the campus. The older frame house had five levels connected by short flights of stairs. There was a garage with a screened in breeze-way leading to the kitchen/dining area. Thank God it had heating and air conditioning, or I might have experienced Patricia's first and only rebellion. While Patricia and her mother enrolled the boys in what was the old Fourth Ward Elementary School, and signed up for utility services, the English professor, who lived next door, and the Head of the Agriculture Department appeared to help us unload the truck. That evening, the English professor's wife brought a hot supper to us. Such volunteered help and friendly hospitality provided great encouragement as we began a new venture. Within the week I turned in the U-Haul van to a dealer in Chattanooga, TN, and took Patricia's parents to Atlanta for their return flight home.

We soon became acquainted with the workers from the Physical Plant Department because the house had its share of maintenance problems. The wiring was not adequate enough to support the expectations of a modern family. One could not use the kitchen oven, clothes washer, and electric clothes dryer at the same time without blowing a fuse. When the Physical Plant Office was called, they always wanted to know which trade was involved, plumbing, electrical, or carpentry? One day, Patricia saw water dripping from an upstairs ceiling light bulb. When asked which trade to send, she said, "Water is coming from an upstairs light bulb! You decide who you want to send!" Both a plumber and an electrician showed up, implying by their actions and demeanor that they were dealing with a crazy woman. They were chagrinned to see that she was telling the truth! A condenser basin in the air conditioning system in the attic space was leaking water which found its way into a ceiling mounted electrical box and followed down to the light bulb.

The Berry house did have adequate interior space, but the yard was not big enough for outdoor games. However there were plenty of recreational opportunities nearby. The boys could walk through "The Crack" to access Berry's open playing fields and Memorial Gym. The Crack was a foot path through the dense pine trees and underbrush acting as a barrier-divider between the campus and Redmond Road on the north side of the Summerville Park residential area. Even closer to the south of the home was a city park with picnic tables and fenced-in tennis courts.

Beginning teaching at Berry

I thought it was odd that I hadn't met the retiring Department Head in all of the interviewing and moving time. The Dean explained that the Department Head's home was in Tennessee. He lived there when school was not in session and rented a room from Berry through the week during school terms. Therefore, he was not available except when he was directly under his nine-month academic contract. Berry's administration had realized that leadership of the Department and participation in the administration required full-time attention, and so had offered me the full-year contract. What the Dean didn't tell me was that he had never discussed my appointment or the understandings related to my contract with the current Department Head. That omission created an unnecessarily awkward relationship to begin the new year when I appeared and introduced myself to him. He had retired from the army as a Colonel, and he was right in his judgment that this was no way to run an organization. It took all of the first semester to win his trust and respect.

I understand that my specific teaching assignments for the term were determined later that day in a heated meeting between the Dean and the Department Head. I wasn't present at the meeting, but the Dean gave me the details. I was to teach a drafting class, a basic electricity class, supervise three student teachers, and fill out the rest of my load by curriculum development. Curriculum development entailed preparing for a new graphic arts course to be offered during the winter quarter in the currently empty space, studying what should be taught in the various majors of the Department, and recommending revised courses and sequences if necessary. He also wanted a long range plan to recruit new students. I was to give my Department Head full respect, but report my progress directly to the Dean. The present Department Head was told he would have to retire in one year at the age of seventy.

I found students who majored in the Department to be practical in their background and interests. There was a mixture of veterans, farm boys, and serious craftsmen. The agriculture students were integrated into many of the Departmental courses. My students were a bit like my first electronic students in New Jersey in that many of them didn't see why they had to learn anything beyond the physical craft skills. I asked them why they were in college if all they wanted to do was saw boards and drive nails. They could do those things without spending four years of their lives in college. I was glad I didn't have to fail a group of them in order to convince them I was serious. Most came to appreciate the high academic standards. Vocabulary, theories, supporting mathematics, and written reports accompanied the practical work as hallmarks of my courses.

Lee R. Clendenning, PhD

Developing graphic arts facilities

I pleaded my case for more resources for the graphic arts program with the Department Head and Dean. Being an old military man, the Head alerted me to the possibilities of getting equipment and supplies through US Government Surplus. There, I was able to obtain equipment and various kinds and sizes of bulk paper. By January, the Department was ready to offer the new graphic arts course. The course became one of the most popular open electives on campus.

Chapter 18

Administering the Industrial Education Department

I knew at my interview that the position of Head of the Department of Industrial Education and Technology at Berry would require everything I had learned and experienced up to that point. I was ready for that challenge. I initially had some reservations about whether committing myself to a small private school would ultimately prove to be a professional dead end. In spite of my qualms, I felt that the "Unseen Hand" had brought me to this point, and I would trust Him to work out any further directions. As events unfolded, I could not have asked for a more supportive environment, or more opportunities for growth than I realized at Berry College. As a Department Head, I became the shepherd of my faculty and students. I was responsible for encouraging the long-term goals of both groups and being sure the pathways and resources necessary to achieve those goals were available. This responsibility included everything from budgeting, procuring materials, security of expensive tools and equipment, maintaining a safe environment, upholding the integrity of the curricula, listening to personnel and personal problems, delivering instruction in assigned courses, and evaluating overall effectiveness of operations to the satisfaction of certification and accreditation agencies. I was solving administrative problems as they arose and learning as much in my own domain as my students were in theirs.

Lee R. Clendenning, PhD

Patricia provides my secretarial services

When I came on board, the Department was served by a competent student secretary. I understood that this was the case with most other academic departments. At a faculty meeting in the following spring, the Dean announced that departments would have to comply with new federal privacy rights. In practical terms, this meant that student secretaries could no longer process documents that contained protected confidential information about other students. Each department would need at least a part-time professional secretary. Small departments could share a secretary. Such secretaries could supervise student assistants in non-confidential tasks.

Following the meeting, the Dean approached me; knowing that Patricia had been assisting me, he asked, "Would Patricia be interested in one of these half-time positions?"

Since the boys were now in school, I thought she probably would, so I answered, "Yes."

Then he said, "My wife would like one of these positions too. Since you will be the Department Head, you can have your choice, my wife, or yours. Whoever you do not take will work for the Physical Education Department."

I was pleasantly surprised. "Well, if I really have a choice, of course, I will take my own wife. We have worked together informally all our married life."

"Good!" he said, and was gone.

For the next several years, Patricia was my official, half-time paid secretary. Patricia became the first person that an enquiring student would encounter as he or she entered the building, and she became the Department's most effective recruiter. Patricia actually worked many more hours than the half-time designator would indicate. In addition to office work and recruiting, she became my best fund raiser, banquet planner, tour bus guide, student listener, and committed Berry representative everywhere she went. (She could sell sand in the desert, or ice to Eskimos!)

Breaking the "Separation of Church and State" barrier

The Supervisor of Industrial Arts for the Georgia Department of Education contacted me as a representative of Berry's Industrial Arts Teacher Preparation Program to request that Berry host summer workshops for in-service teachers to implement the new courses, "The World of Manufacturing," and "The World of Construction." These junior high courses had been developed with a federal grant by the Department of Industrial Arts at Ohio State University. To keep our program up to date, Berry sent me to a special workshop for professors at Ohio State University to become fully qualified to direct such workshops. But, I discovered that the Georgia Department of Education would not actually fund workshops at Berry because of our non-denominational Christian foundation. They were concerned about "Separation of Church and State," and so expected Berry to offer and support the workshops without state or federal funding. That didn't seem fair to me.

Doing some basic research, I discovered that Berry was producing more industrial arts teachers for the state than the three State institutions—the University of Georgia, Savannah State College, and Georgia Southern College—at a time when there was a great shortage of such teachers. I discussed the situation with the State Supervisor of Industrial Arts, who said that he regretted it; but the decision was made "above him." I asked him if I provided proof that Berry could conduct such workshops without religious indoctrination or discrimination of any kind, would he present the information to the "powers that be" and appeal the decision. He replied that he could not promise anything, but it would not hurt to present the argument.

I gathered copies of Berry's documents describing non-discrimination in hiring and student admissions policies as well as statistics showing the numbers of minority faculty and students, both by race and declared religion. The numbers outside the main stream were admittedly small, but enough to support my argument. I also obtained published statements describing the classes taught in the Department of Religion as being purely academic studies of religious viewpoints and heritages rather than promotions of any particular doctrines. I also showed that Berry was controlled independently of any church or denomination. The church on campus served the campus population, but it in no way governed the institution.

With my facts as background, I wrote a letter of appeal to the State Supervisor including permission to share the letter with his superiors. I used a three-pronged argument: (1) There was no church from which to be separated. (2) State and federal funds could be used in the Berry environment without fear of religious indoctrination or discrimination of any kind. (3) Expecting Berry, as a private, non-profit institution, to continue to compete with State-funded institutions in fulfilling the critical need for up-to-date teachers in this field was unrealistic. Without a more even playing field, Berry would eventually be forced to discontinue the program, and the State would need to more than double its capacity to produce such teachers.

The letter apparently reached the right individuals. I soon received word that the State Supervisor was authorized to fund The World of Construction Workshop at Berry at the same level as the state institutions. To my knowledge, the propriety of state and federal funding of workshops, Job Corps Training programs, and requests for proposals (RFP's) for contractual work at Berry College was never questioned again. Until Berry closed the Industrial Education Department in the early 1990s, I administered state-funded workshops and fulfilled curriculum writing contracts every year. The Berry Home Economics program and, later, the Berry Department of Education, started State funded activities.

Dealing with Recruited Minorities

My main idea for the required recruitment plan was to expand enrollment of females and minority students into the Department. The foundation for success of such a plan was already present. In answer to one of my questions about racial prejudice in my interview, the President had been proud of the fact that Berry, under his leadership, had been able to integrate the races within the student body without serious incident. In fact, the current Director of Financial Aid was a black man. There was one black student athlete enrolled in the Department. I was pleased to discover two very serious and competent female students in my first drafting class. They were the pioneering examples of success I needed. The Director of Admissions agreed to divert some of his recruitment budget to cover travel for me to visit public school counselors and industrial arts teachers in senior high schools in chosen districts around the state. This support, along with descriptive pamphlets which I designed and printed, continued to grow enrollment for a number of years.

A black student columnist for the Berry student newspaper, *The Campus Carrier*, who was interested in taking the graphic arts course, stopped into Patricia's office to ask questions. He was openly concerned that he would be discriminated against by a biased instructor. Patricia answered all his questions and tried to reassure him that I would treat him fairly. He enrolled and was making good progress in the course. When he had to use the offset press for the first time, like most of my students, he made a mess of black ink setting up the press for his job. He had not cleaned his hands as he reached for a ream of new, bright white paper to put in the press.

Without thinking about my words, or my audience, I called across the lab to him just as I would to any other student. "Halsey, don't you reach for that clean paper with your black hands!"

He stopped and looked at me as if I was from Mars. "Dr. Clendenning," he said, holding out both bare hands, looking down at them. "It doesn't rub off, honest!"

I choked back my laughter. "Turn your hands over," I commanded. He looked puzzled, but did as I commanded; revealing black ink smudges on palm pads and finger tips. "That is the black I was worried about," I said. He became my friend.

A few of the black students were athletes who had played out their eligibility without completing graduation requirements. When their athletic scholarships were exhausted, they came to the Department seeking help. Over the years, I was able to help a few of them by calling the Rome Boy's Club and setting up paid internships as coaching assistants and/or craft teachers. I was able to employ a couple doing clean-up within the Department. One tall basketball hero became a director of a Boy's Club within his home city.

We were also successful in recruitment of female students. A few of them were militant feminists who objected to being referred to as "girls." That was understandable, and I made a conscious effort to use the term "women" when referring to them collectively. I was giving a lecture on electric welding theory, safety, and general procedures one day in advance of actual demonstration and practice in the lab. In describing the process, I said that they would learn to listen to the electric arc as well as watch it through their face shields.

One of the women asked me, "What does the arc sound like?"

"It sizzles and fries like an egg broken into a very hot skillet," I replied.

I was surprised when my Associate Dean later called me into his office and informed me that I had been accused of "talking down" to my women students. In the future, I was not to use "domestic analogies" in my lectures.

One day, a couple of women came to me complaining that their instructor was using "sexist and nasty" terms. "What terms are you talking about?" I inquired.

One replied, "He talks about male and female threads when he could just as easily say inside and outside threads."

The other added, "Just because he does not like a particular file, he doesn't have to call it a bastard."

I explained that these were perfectly respectable terms used in many trades. I yanked a tool catalog from my shelf and showed them the page listing the "Bastard" file. I also showed them catalog pages which specified matching male and female parts.

They were not impressed and seriously proposed, "We should change the language to make it sexist free."

I shifted gears. "You are pioneers, breaking into what has traditionally been a male domain. As you graduate and move into those jobs, you will need to understand the language to be successful. If you react oddly every time someone uses a term which has other meanings in other situations, people will wonder where your mind wanders. We are one, small program in a big universe. We are in no position to change the world. Your instructor is simply using the language of the shops." Seeing the look of skepticism on their faces, I added, "You don't have to like it. Just live with it." The last remark seemed to help.

The shop restroom facilities had been designed for males, including a shower stall and changing area. The only female restroom was a small closet converted to accommodate a secretary. I thoroughly antagonized my male students and staff by converting their woodworking glue room into a modern facility for the larger numbers of female students.

Establishing Gender-Free Safety Standards

For the student's protection, I had to develop a safety dress code which was gender neutral in description and enforcement. Of course, impact resistant safety glasses led the list. Exposed skin on feet, legs, and upper arms had to be covered, and hair could not impede vision. Work in the foundry had additional, specialized equipment and rules for dealing with quantities of molten metal. Physical guards were to be used on woodworking machines. My rules ran counter to the prevalent culture which was accepting long hair for males and encouraging individual freedom of expression with increasing skin exposure. Surprisingly, the males gave me more problems than the females. They didn't like safety glasses or guards.

Dealing with Campus Politics

When I arrived on campus I had no idea that a segment of the faculty felt that the college should be governed collectively by the teaching faculty. By listening at the monthly meetings of the Faculty Council, I also discovered that there had been only minimal faculty raises in recent years. The Faculty Council meetings lasted overtime as individuals avidly talked to a captive audience. Additional special meetings were called to provide more time for discussion about the possibility of forming a faculty union.

The majority of the faculty, though also concerned about their salaries, realized the institution was facing serious financial problems and trusted that that the administration was trying to address those problems. Many of us felt we had to attend all meetings in order to assure that the body would not pass motions of "no confidence," or worse, that would only complicate the problems. I was not bashful about addressing nonsense when I heard it. I had observed the difference in efficiency between union labor and non-union labor in the construction field, so I didn't want a union representative speaking for me. In the spring, when the time came to elect a new Faculty Council Chairman, I was surprised to be nominated and elected, along with sensible supporting officers.

In the fall, I instituted one major change in conducting the Council meetings. Remembering my seventh grade training in 4-H, I decided to strictly follow and enforce parliamentary procedure, a requirement in the By-Laws of the organization, which apparently had never been enforced. That reduced most verbal input to either making a motion, seconding a motion, speaking in support of or against a seconded motion when recognized, or raising parliamentary questions. Some of the professors of history, English, and political science, as well as a few sympathizers, who should have applauded this change, were strongly opposed to it. They wanted "free" discussion and felt that I was muzzling them. I had the support of the majority of the faculty. The next Council meeting lasted only eighteen minutes, I guess setting a record. In addition to saving a lot of meeting time, the group learned how to accomplish necessary business efficiently.

Dissident faculty did bring civil lawsuits and launched complaints of unfair labor practices with the federal authorities against the administration. After my term as Council Chairperson ended, I was appointed to chair the Faculty Hearing Committee charged with hearing complaints, fact-finding, and making recommendations to the Administration. I was threatened with a lawsuit, but none was ever actually filed against me. Collateral damage from the legal struggles at Berry included an unfortunate administrative shake-up. The Dean who hired me left to accept a good position elsewhere. Some Department Chairs were rearranged, and mistrust between some faculty and the administration continued for years. On the positive side, department chairs supportive of the administration were appointed and their legal positions and roles clarified. Early on, I had been assigned a very competent woman, Dr. Ouida Dickey, as my Associate Dean. She was a Berry graduate with a strong background in business and economics education and became a long-time professional friend. In years to follow, I served with her on many committees and task forces. The first such assignment was to screen candidates for the replacement Dean/Academic Vice President. After he was on board, with his encouragement, we tackled the General Education requirements. I am proud to say that the basic structure we designed stood the test of four Southern Association of Schools and Colleges accreditation evaluations and almost forty years of efforts to revise by those who thought they could improve it.

Chapter 19

Taking Care of the Family

Berry's campus with its resources was a wonderful place to raise children. We explored every location from the main highway to the House of Dreams at the top of Lavender Mountain, walking the trails and riding bicycles on the backwoods roads. We played tennis on the courts, swam in the pool, and the boys played pick-up basketball most anytime they were free. But, not all of our efforts to encourage family togetherness worked out as envisioned.

Fishing promotes family togetherness?

I had always heard about the family values of taking children fishing. Since we observed many people fishing along the shores of beautiful Victory Lake, I decided it was time to try fishing with the family. I purchased four poles, mounted casting reels, and attached hooks, leaders, and floating bobbers according to the recommendations of a salesman at a local sporting goods store. All was loaded into the station wagon, and off we went! We parked on the shore where I had observed people fishing on other occasions. With excited anticipation and high hopes, the hooks were baited, and we started drowning worms.

The lake was shallow with lots of vegetation, bushes, and tree roots in the water and along the shore. The boys immediately started snagging the hooks, sometimes behind them, sometimes on something under the water, sometimes with each other's lines. Worms seemed to disappear and needed replacing without any sense of fish being to blame. I spent my time solving problems and trying to provide instruction in an activity in which I had never had any success, even on trout streams on the home farm. After a couple of hours in the hot Georgia sun without a real nibble for any of us, everybody's patience wore out, and we put the poles back in the wagon. Before climbing in ourselves, we stood for a minute looking over the smooth, pretty water.

In frustration, Patricia said, "There's no fish in that lake anyway!"

BOOM! And the ground beneath us shuddered! All over that lake, fish flipped through the surface in unison. The explosion was a blast in a stone quarry not far as the crow flies from the lake. There were plenty of fish there; they either didn't like our bait or our technique. Somehow, I never did get back to fishing.

(Addendum: During his college days, Richard went with friends on a fishing trip to one of many commercial fishing ponds scattered around the State of Georgia. When I asked him if he had any better luck than we had at Victory Lake, he said, "Dad, you wouldn't believe it! Those fish were so eager to be caught that we had to hide behind a tree in order to bait the hook.)

Chip and Richard's fun

The Rome area offered many opportunities for organized physical activities for growing boys. Chip and Richard participated in age appropriate activities sponsored by the Rome Boys Club and the Rome-Floyd County Recreation Authority. There were teams and competitions in baseball, basketball, and soccer. Individual competitions included wrestling, and ping pong. Practices and competitions were generally after school, and on Saturday mornings. For most events, Patricia and I arranged our work schedules to be cheering on the sidelines. Although at this age our boys were not outstanding performers, they had success enough to gain confidence and appreciate the value of trying their best.

Chip (and later Richard) became a student crossing guard for West Central Elementary School, so he had to be delivered to his assigned intersection early each morning. These assignments provided good training in responsibility.

Left, Lee, Jr (Chip) & Richard

Chapter 20

People to People Goodwill Ambassador for Vocational Education— Europe and Russia

The Invitation to be a People to People Goodwill Ambassador for Vocational Education came as a complete surprise. I had been active in professional and honorary organizations since undergraduate days. At Berry, I was supported with travel funds to continue attending state, regional, national and international events within this country. As the Berry College Trustee of the local chapter of Epsilon Pi Tau, the honorary society for industrial arts and vocational education professionals, I became, responsible for all operations, including recruitment of top level speakers at our Annual Banquet. Leaders in our disciplines from across the country were intrigued by Berry's program and facilities. I acquired many professional friends. Still, I was as surprised as anyone in the winter of 1976 when I was one of the professors to receive an invitation to become part of the delegation being assembled at the University of Wisconsin by Dr. Merle Strong (whom I did not personally know). I learned that the People to People Goodwill Organization had been founded by President Dwight Eisenhower to encourage communication and understanding between lay people in various nations. During the height of the Cold

War, opportunities for lay Americans to get behind the Russian Iron Curtain were greatly restricted. A portion of my invitation explained the purpose of this mission:

> To give the vocational leaders in the United States an opportunity to carry a message of goodwill to their occupational counterparts in Europe and the Soviet Union. To see and inspect, in person, typical vocational educational institutions; to learn and compare methods and procedures, and to have an enjoyable holiday visiting with and being guests of the people who make up the delegates' occupational counterparts in these countries. This mission is an official program of People to People International, with headquarters in Kansas City, Missouri.

Berry was very supportive of my Goodwill opportunity. The administration approved a Faculty Development Grant which covered much of my overseas travel expenses and continued my salary while I was gone. The College also supplied me with descriptive brochures and imprinted ball-point pens to be shared with the people I would meet. Each delegate was allowed to invite a spouse or close friend to accompany him or her; however, a spouse's or friend's expenses were not covered either by People to People or the College. I was not going to go without Patricia, so we had to find the funds for her travel, photographic film, and other tourist incidentals. We also had to arrange for Patricia's parents in Fabius, New York, to look after the boys for our extended absence. I modified any other plans for the coming summer and concentrated on applying for passports and visas, and other details in order to go. I thanked the Lord for the chance of a lifetime He had dropped into my lap.

We are off!

We joined our delegation in New York City, met everybody, and learned what was expected in an orientation session. Twenty of us were to travel first to Amsterdam, Holland, by way of London, then to Copenhagen, Denmark, and on to Malmo and Stockholm, Sweden. From there we were to go by ship to Helsinki, Finland and to travel by train into Leningrad (now St. Petersburg), Russia. From Leningrad, the famous Red Arrow Express Train was to take us into Moscow. Our last major stop would be Munich, Germany, before returning to New York. In each country we were to meet U. S. Ambassadors or high level personnel from the Department of State, Ministers of Education, college professors, and instructional level counterparts. In addition, we were scheduled to visit local vocational-technical schools and a few of the local tourist attractions.

Holland

We must have landed at the height of the tulip season in Amsterdam, Holland. Whole fields, seemingly as big as our wheat fields, were covered in beautiful colors. As we rode in our tour bus, I was startled to look out the window at an ocean-going passenger liner sailing through a field of tulips. The canal the ship was floating in was too low to be seen.

We stayed in a hotel just down the street from the house where Anne Frank, the Jewish refugee from the Nazis, had hidden. In front of the hotel, a narrow street ran parallel to another canal. As we sat at our first meal there, the table started shifting around. We could feel our chairs move up and down. The guide said, "Don't be alarmed; that's only a barge passing on the canal. The foundations shift around as the water changes wave pressures." Interested in structure, I asked, "How has the building held together all these years with a shifting foundation?" He said, "The foundation of the building is a boat structure that is floating in thick mud. As boats pass, they displace the canal water creating shifting pressure and movement of the mud."

Later, we took a boat tour on the canal "highway" system. There were traffic lights at intersections and windmills running pumps to control water levels. We passed through a large residential section where the sides of the canal accommodated permanently anchored "house" barges. People who lived there had waterside mail boxes and beautiful flower gardens on deck surrounding their living quarters. I was intrigued that some of the floating barges were constructed with steel-reinforced concrete. Previous to our actual tour, I had assumed that Holland's dike system was limited to claiming agricultural land from the sea. Our visit revealed that water control is vital to the way of life and culture of vast, non-agricultural regions of the Netherlands.

The North Sea community of Volendam was our best tourist stop in the Netherlands. The Dutch hot chocolate was wonderful, the windmills picturesque, and the wooden shoe factory educational for a woodworker like me. I tried on a wooden shoe; however, they seemed too uncomfortable for me to spend money on, even as a souvenir.

In The Hague, we met with the Chief Inspector of Education for the Netherlands. I was impressed to be where so much international diplomacy, such as the League of Nations, has occurred. We enjoyed lunch with the Ambassador from the United States and more personnel from the Dutch Ministry of Education. We experienced an Indonesian Buffet Dinner (Indonesia used to be a Dutch colony) where Patricia and I enjoyed the food once we identified what was monkey meat so that we could avoid it. We did not ask the identity of some of the other menu items.

In our first meeting of counterparts, we learned that the Dutch secondary school system, like the other European countries we would visit, had only two main tracks. The academic program prepared students for the university, and the vocational program prepared students for skilled trade and technical occupations. There were no "General Education" programs as we had in this country to serve "undecided" students. They tried to convince us that there were no undecided students. Vocational programs were greatly influenced by trade unions and guilds which strongly influenced generations of students to follow in their parents' path. We visited vocational programs with first class facilities in the areas of restaurant cooking and graphic arts. They would have been what we would expect to find in our best post-secondary training programs.

Denmark

We flew to Copenhagen, Denmark, in a 747. The first attraction was a boat tour of the harbor sailing close to the city and National government buildings. The real highlight of the water tour was seeing the statue of the "Little Mermaid by the Sea," famous from the writings of Hans Christian Anderson, and looking as if she had just emerged from the water. Later, we also visited the interiors of the government buildings and Royal Palaces.

Learning how to gamble

One evening in Copenhagen, our group went into the entertainment section of the Tivoli Gardens. The Gardens appeared to be the major tourist attraction of the city featuring acres of flowered walking trails, restaurants, family amusement areas, and gambling attractions, sort of a combination of Callaway Gardens, Disney Land, and Las Vegas. As we were strolling past the one-armed bandit slot machines, someone in our party handed Patricia a gambling token and insisted that she put it in the nearest machine and pull the handle. She wanted no part of the activity, but their persistence prevailed. When she yanked the handle, Whirl! Klang! Bang! The machine started spitting out tokens, each one about the size of a US quarter. I cupped my hands and caught them. When we started to move on, more of the party stopped us and insisted that Patricia put one of the tokens back into the machine. No way! They were now hers, and she was not going to part with a one!

"Why put one back?" I asked.

"Look at the machine," someone said. "It is showing three matching pictures. That means it has just paid off a winner. No one else will gamble with a machine which has just paid off. It is common courtesy to put one of the tokens back and pull the handle so that others will use the machine."

Patricia still would not put a token back, so someone else did. In the morning, I took the handful of tokens back to the Gardens and cashed them in for about twelve US dollars.

Lee R. Clendenning, PhD

Real Sharing with a Counterpart

At one of the scheduled dinner parties in the evening, we were assigned seating paired with the spouses of our counterparts. Patricia's dinner partner spoke English; however, his wife, my partner, was too timid to hardly try. When we discovered that they were as uncomfortable in the contrived situation as we were, as soon as we gracefully could, we became a four-some party. They relaxed, and we talked about families, bowling, and schools. We left the larger party and continued our fellowship during a walk through a lighted section of the Garden. It was a nice evening, and they were really down to earth people. The walk through the lighted Gardens with new friends, followed by a fireworks display, finished off a perfect evening.

School and church visits

We toured the National Institute for Vocational Education, the Mechanical Engineering Department of the Technical University of Denmark, and the Commercial College of Copenhagen. The Institute was an office complex with associated meeting rooms for lectures. Danish educational officials met us there and described their programs, which were not remarkably different from those in the other Northern European countries. The Technical University was very modern in architecture, but traditional in drafting facilities. Patricia, a professional secretary, was most interested in the Commercial College where students prepared to be teachers of standard office skills. There were typing laboratories, office machine centers, and telephone receptionist training stations.

An interesting lecture on religion and church life in Denmark was presented at the Grundtrigs Church. This modern structure had a long narrow sanctuary with an extremely high vaulted ceiling. I was disappointed to hear that only a small percentage of the population worshiped anywhere, in Denmark. Lutherans were the most active group described, however the bulk of the younger generation was described as secular.

Sweden

On our way from Copenhagen, Denmark to Malmo, Sweden, we skimmed the waters of a passageway between the North Sea and the Baltic Sea in a hydrofoil boat. As we entered, the interior of the boat looked like any other small commercial passenger craft. Seating was wrapped in a semi-circle around the front of the boat with a glass windshield for sightseeing and protection on three sides. As the boat picked up speed, it rose above the water; riding on what looked like big water-skis. The boat cruised at approximately fifty miles an hour, and the ride was really quiet and smooth. We could walk around a service island in the middle of the boat where refreshments were sold.

Arriving in Malmo, a bus ride through open countryside with apple trees in blossom took us to the University of Lund campus. The many buildings were spread out, separated by well-manicured lawns and shade trees. There, we visited another small church, an art museum, and one public school. The children at the school could have been mistaken for typical American students except for the strange sounding language. After a return to Malmo, Patricia and I visited a modern Swedish furniture design center within walking distance of the hotel. The design of the furniture featured close grained hardwoods, simple structure as expected in Danish pieces, smooth satin finishes, and superb craftsmanship. We spent the night and boarded a plane for Stockholm, Sweden, in the morning.

The first day in Stockholm, we visited Vastberga Gymnasium (high school), ate lunch at the hotel, and caught up on some needed sleep in the afternoon. The evening dinner with Swedish guests was at Stallmastare-Garden, the oldest restaurant in Sweden. The domestic reindeer steaks were delicious! By this time, Patricia and I were becoming the preferred dinner partners of those who enjoyed alcoholic drinks of various kinds. They had discovered that we would not touch ours, so whoever was close received a double ration. Tea, soft drinks, coffee, and water were always available for us.

That evening at 10:30, local time, we called Chip and Richard to let them know we were still on earth, and to be sure they were all right. They were fine, but still seemed glad to hear from us. Back then, the long distance call of short duration cost $25.00. The modern internet provides much cheaper communication.

The following day, our anniversary, we toured the Stockholm harbor and water-front by boat. As in Copenhagen, the government buildings and King's Palace were built right at the edge of the water. Back on land, we visited the church where their young king, Carl XVI Gustaf, was to be married later in the month. Sweden celebrates its National Day on June 6th. This is the date on which Gustav Vasa was crowned king in 1523, and on which a new constitution was adopted in 1809. We had the opportunity to watch a parade with children dressed in colorful native style and carrying flags and flowers. Later that evening, we enjoyed another formal dinner with high level educational personnel. They described the efforts of the Swedish government to bring modern education to remote locations in Lapland. Traditionally, Laplander's education entailed only learning survival skills passed on from generation to generation. With the Internet and satellite communication, I imagine reaching into Lapland would be much easier today.

Finland

From Stockholm, we rode to Helsinki, Finland in an overnight steamer big enough to load railroad cars into the hold. On board in the evening we enjoyed a genuine Swedish smorgasbord, which had an endless variety of delicious choices. I can say that I have eaten genuine Swedish meatballs! However, if one hesitated to take a picture, or went back for something missed on the serving line, the workers bussing the tables grabbed the plate; and the food was gone! As in American buffets, a clean plate was to be used each time one returned to the food serving area.

To spend the night in the ship, we were assigned a nice stateroom with a porthole window. The ship was so quiet and smooth that Patricia repeatedly thought it had stalled. She would wake up, go to the window to check that scenery was passing, and return to bed. She could see out because we were far enough north, and near enough to the longest day of the year, to be in twilight all night long.

In Helsinki, we toured by bus the first morning, seeing the Olympic Stadium and the rest of the city. Back at the hotel, letters from Chip, Richard, and Patricia's mother caught up with us. They reassured us that they were OK, playing golf in the back yard when they were not riding around the region with their grandfather. It was good to hear from them. The evening formal dinner included nine guests from the Finland Ministry of Education and a representative of the US Embassy Consulate to Finland. They loaded us with official literature describing all aspects of the Finnish educational system. By now, we had enough literature and souvenirs to warrant shipping a box home to lighten our travel load.

Walking back to the hotel with the group after the formal dinner, Patricia and I decided to have a little fun. She avoids elevators if possible. The one in our vintage hotel was unusually slow and surrounded by a staircase with two intermediate landings around the back corners between each floor. All of the tour group's rooms were on the eighth floor. As the group approached the elevator, someone punched the up button for service. I said, "We will meet you folks upstairs." We climbed as fast as we could to the next floor, pushed the service request button, and ran for the next floor, repeating the process all the way up. At the eighth floor, we gathered our breath quickly and stood in front of the elevator door waiting for our group.

When the door opened, we innocently said, "What detained you?"

Somebody replied, "This dumb elevator stopped at every floor, even though there was no one to get on!"

We never told the group what we did, but have enjoyed the secret between us to this day.

Spending a final day in Helsinki, we met more personnel from the Ministry of Education and toured two vocational schools. The new comprehensive vocational school, which cost nine million dollars to build, was very impressive with its polished stone exterior and floors. It was obviously built with influence from new American vocational schools being built at that time. The laboratories and classroom layouts were structured for group classes rather than the individual instruction which characterized the older apprenticeship system. The Hotel and Restaurant Planning and Training School was the most unique one we visited because it mixed modern laboratories and cooking equipment for group instruction with individual tutoring in the culinary arts. We enjoyed watching the training class prepare the meal they served us later.

Rules for Entering Russia

That evening, at a group meeting before boarding the train from Helsinki to Leningrad, Russia, we were instructed on the special rules we were to observe in the USSR. We were told we would be secretly observed and bugged for sound from the time we boarded the train until we left Russia. We were not to talk among ourselves about anything of national importance. All money entering and leaving the country had to be accounted for to the penny on government forms, even money which might be exchanged between spouses. To avoid the black market, currency was only to be exchanged at officially designated places. We were to ask permission before taking any pictures. Pictures from high places overlooking scenic views, rivers, city skylines, or any view that might have military value were especially forbidden. Personal Bibles were acceptable; any other religious or political literature was subject to seizure. Our Russian tour guide was to know our locations at all times. We were not to leave the group to explore on our own. Attendance would be taken at all scheduled events, and we were to report on time. Finally, to avoid the spread of harmful insects, no fresh fruit of any kind was to be taken into the USSR. The penalties for violations of any of these rules could mean detention in Russia until the charges against the guilty party could be settled. We were also told that there were some border misunderstandings between Finland and Russia, but the issues should not concern us.

Even though it was past 9:00 p.m., it was still daylight outdoors as we excitedly boarded the train for our next adventure. The train cars had a hallway on one side of each car with windows. Berths were assigned to pairs of travelers.

After settling our baggage in our berth, Patricia and I went back into the hallway to see what might be going on. A home economics professor from Bellingham, Washington, was upset because she had just remembered a fresh grapefruit was in her luggage. Always the problem solver, I said, "Bring it to me." I opened the car window and quietly dropped the grapefruit straight down. A man walking on the platform between our train and the next one hollered something to me, shook his head and finger at me, put down his briefcase, climbed down from the platform to the track level, picked up the fruit, and threw it back in the window. After shaking his finger at me again, he picked up his briefcase and walked on. OK, I had committed a "NO NO"! She tried to give the fruit to the observer at the front of our car. He would have no part of it. After the train was going about fifty-miles-per-hour through the Finnish countryside, I knew we could get rid of the incriminating fruit. Agreeing with me, a fellow traveler threw it out the window. It did not come back!

Excitement near the Russian boarder

After watching the countryside go by for a while, Patricia and I retired for the evening. The train stopped briefly a couple of times. Suddenly, it came to a screeching halt. I roused enough to peek out the berth window. In the twilight, what looked like a platoon of soldiers with assault weapons came rushing out of the woods toward the train.

Patricia took a look. "Get back down!" I told her. "I don't know what is going on."

After being stalled for over half an hour, the train continued on. Before long, we heard voices and commotion in the next berth. We got up to see what was happening. Our new friend from Bellingham had been summoned to the front of the train. She told the following story which sounds like a scene from a B movie.

A paper mill engineer from Bellingham, Washington, was involved in a pulpwood business which required periodic travel between Finland and Russia. For whatever reason, he had missed boarding the train in Helsinki and had tried to catch up with it by taxi at one of the stops we had made. At that location, he was again too late to board properly, but had run and jumped onto the rear of the last car as the train was leaving. After riding outside, hanging on for some time, he was spotted. The train was stopped, and a local military detachment was alerted. As his papers were being cleared, he was told that there was a woman, also from Bellingham, on board. She was brought forward, ostensibly to meet him.

Apparently, the coincidental meeting of two people from Bellingham raised some suspicions among the Russians. After we crossed the border at 5:00 a.m., Russian customs agents came through the train checking our visas, passports, luggage, and currency statements. Our friend from Bellingham was the only person to have her luggage unpacked completely and every garment thoroughly inspected.

Russia

As a result of the eventful night, we arrived in Leningrad completely exhausted and not really ready to appreciate the full day of activities planned for us. Our first impression of Russia was one of surprise at the lack of color and cheerfulness everywhere we looked. The contrast with the late spring blooming of flowers in window boxes and smiling people wearing a mixture of styles and colors of clothing in the European countries we had visited was striking. Here, no flowers were in sight. The people, with what seemed like sad facial expressions and all wearing gray to dark colored clothing, looked down as they trudged the streets. Many of the buildings were obviously built following the same set of blue-prints featuring mostly unfinished grey concrete with too many cracks and crumbles. The streets and sidewalks were kept spotlessly clean by older ladies who could be seen on many blocks with their brooms and dustpans. They and the uniformed police on most street

Revealing the Unseen Hand

corners were apparently part of the reason that the Communists bragged that there was no unemployment in their system.

The first stop was the hotel where our passports were confiscated with the promise that we could have them returned when we checked out. The official at the main desk gave each of us a slip of paper with our floor and room number assignment. A watcher was assigned to each floor with a small desk beside the elevator door. Shown the room assignment slip, the floor watcher handed out the proper key. We could not leave the floor for any reason without surrendering our key

After breakfast at the hotel, we took an escorted private bus tour of the city. In addition to our assigned guide/interpreter, there were three other Russian travelers sitting near the front, middle, and rear of the bus. They were never introduced to us, and their presence was never explained. We assumed they were some kind of official observers. Although they were not always the same people, we were accompanied on every bus tour we took, both in Leningrad and Moscow. Later, in Moscow, after quiet speculation within the group regarding the role of our silent companions, one gregarious member of our party said, "Watch their faces on the next trip. I will prove to you that they understand English very well." On that trip during a break in the narration, he loudly told a hilarious joke. (I wish I could remember it.) We almost rolled out of our seats laughing. Our fellow Russian travelers were choking to keep their faces straight!

We then went to the luxurious Winter Palace of the Tsars, which had been converted into a fantastic art museum. By then, some in the group were so tired that they began sitting in the ancient chairs along the wall when the narrator stopped to explain a particular feature. They were sternly warned that the chairs were part of the exhibits, and they were not to sit in them. Patricia and I had not committed that "No No!"

The Summer Gardens of Peter the Great, designed after those he had seen in Versailles in France, were in full bloom and beautiful. The flowers were in the center of circular intersections of stone paved walkways, lined by trimmed green hedges.

Back at the hotel in the restaurant for the evening meal, we had an example of one difference between the American and the Russian systems. Rather than a waiter or waitress taking our orders, they had "work orders" detailing what was to be served. They put bottles of beer and soft drinks in the center of each table. The people at our table all happened to be total abstainers. Patricia took our beer and traded it for more soft drink from the next table, which pleased those folks. The waiter saw her do it and came over shaking his head and finger at her. He traded the bottles back the way he had set them originally and stood back watching us from what I assumed to be the kitchen doorway. Later, as the meal progressed, we were able to quietly make the swap without attracting further attention. One lady in our party had a stomach ulcer. Through the interpreter, she requested a glass of milk. The answer came back that our waiter could not serve her milk because milk was not on his work order. Thinking it was an issue of payment, she offered to order milk separately from the tour party and pay for it herself. The waiter was not authorized to take orders that way. Our guide said he would work on the request. She finally was served her milk with the breakfast order the following morning.

The entertainment for the evening was Russian folk singing and dancing at the Mariinsky Theatre, a large concert hall. We were in the best seats in the house, front and center. The costumes were beautiful, the music wonderful, and the dancing unique to that culture. The nature of the male Cossack dancing can be seen in the musical *Fiddler on the Roof.* Our only problem was fatigue. The wife of an older member of our party liked her alcohol which apparently did not help; she repeatedly fell asleep, snoring loudly with her head back. Her husband would wake her up each time, but we were embarrassed. A couple of times, the performers also heard her and scowled when they were supposed to be the picture of cheer. Her behavior didn't dispel the European stereotype of the ugly American on our Goodwill tour.

The following morning, we met with a representative of the Russian Ministry of Education who explained their Polytechnic Education system. This sounded like engineering education in America, ten years previous. Civil and mechanical engineering principles have not changed in years, but their electronics instruction was still based on vacuum tubes rather than solid state physics. I learned that the Russian education system strongly supported oral recitation as an alternative to written responses. My gifts of thirty-five cent ball point pens, which Berry had supplied, were well received. I was told that it was all right for my hosts to accept the pens, but in Russia, pens were only for sale on the black market for $12.00 each. Pencils and newsprint quality paper were readily available. No explanation for the reluctance to make pens available was provided. I thought maybe the Communists were afraid that "the pen is mightier than the sword."

Before lunch, we toured beautiful St. Isaac's Cathedral, which the Communists had turned into a structural museum. Much of the contents of the building that would have had religious significance had been replaced by displays of the methods of construction. The building took forty years to be completed and occupied a whole city block. It was supported with polished marble walls and columns topped by a gold-plated dome. The gold was first dissolved in mercury, which was then painted on the roof surface. Torches were used to boil away the mercury leaving the gold coating. Approximately sixty volunteer workers a day sacrificed their lives to the poisonous mercury vapors.

Apparently, the Communists did not completely succeed in erasing the religious significance of the building. There was a line of people waiting to enter stretching half way around the block. In this "classless" society, we were ushered into a side door away from the waiting people. Following our guide, I felt bad to be forced to crash the line of people already in the building making their way through the allowed tourist path. Many of them had tears streaming down their cheeks. To an outside observer, they appeared to behave more like pilgrims than tourists. I concluded that religion was not as dead in the USSR as we had been led to believe.

In the Russian secondary trade school we visited after lunch, the walls of each shop were covered with illustrations of the procedures to be followed. Except for language, the illustrations could have been large scale reproductions of the overhead transparencies used to teach the same tasks in the US. I was granted permission to photograph the posters. I guess I was too deeply engrossed in my task, because suddenly I heard a loud "CLICK." Looking around, the entire party had left the room, and our school host had locked the door. I went to the door and pounded until someone came to let me out. The Russians had left me in there until Patricia became concerned about me. Leaving me behind was apparently their method of teaching me a lesson. As I came out, our Russian hosts just gave me dirty looks; but nothing was said. From then on, I stayed closer to the group.

That day, we were also allowed to walk through what was called a Russian Department Store housed in a long building with department booths on both sides monitored by one sales clerk per booth. In the back of each booth, the merchandize was hung on walls or placed on shelves. I'll bet they didn't have a problem with shop-lifting! We were not to buy anything with American money. Foreigners without exchanged funds were only allowed to shop at special stores that were authorized to accept western currencies and credit cards.

Our evening meal was delicious pancakes at what appeared to be a high class restaurant. There were other foreign groups present from European countries. The restaurant featured a multi-piece entertainment band playing pleasant Russian music, like the background for the film *Doctor Zhivago*. We were seated relatively close to the band. Like other evening meal functions with live music, at the end of a number, I never know whether I am expected to clap, or keep eating. I often do some of both. After a few numbers, the band members stalked off with grim faces. Our guide explained that the audience had not expressed enough appreciation. If they really liked a performance, a Russian audience would all clap in rhythmic unison. Maybe it is difficult for ignorant people to spread goodwill.

At midnight, we left Leningrad for Moscow aboard the famous Red Arrow Express train. I enjoyed watching the large agricultural fields and white birch forests in the twilight for a while before retiring to our compartment. We arrived at the Leningrad Hotel in the city of Moscow about 9:00 a.m. The hotel was architecturally identical to the one in Leningrad and operated by the same procedural rules. The room we were assigned was large, with a big chandelier hanging from the center of the ceiling and a patch of greenery growing in a big plant stand in one corner.

We were about to learn that the distrust associated with the Cold War was continuing. After settling luggage and eating breakfast, we started a tour of the Exposition of Progress. It was a huge complex with very informative exhibits extolling USSR accomplishments in many phases of life from stone quarry operations to space exploration. I could have happily spent all day there. We were reminded that we must ask permission before taking a picture of any particular exhibit of interest. Our American leader, Dr. Merle Strong, who was small of stature, had obtained permission for a picture at one exhibit. As he was focusing his camera, he suddenly found himself looking into the chest of a big official who had stepped right in front of him. Dr. Strong started looking upward to see the man's face as I would have gazed upward at the California redwoods. The official grabbed the camera, tore out the roll of film, and handed the camera back to Dr. Strong. There had apparently been some miscommunication at some level, because we were whisked back to the hotel without any explanation. The saved time gave Patricia and me a chance to write home.

We took a tour of the city after lunch. One of our fellow travelers apparently enjoyed the lunch beverage too much, and promptly went to sleep. Everywhere we stopped for an allowed picture, I picked up his camera and also clicked one for him. Reminiscing with me years later at a convention, he said, "I went home and showed my pictures to my wife. You know, I don't actually remember seeing half that stuff we saw in Moscow." I smiled inwardly, but didn't confess what I had done.

Our tour took us to Lenin Hills, overlooking the city, the Volga River, and the Kremlin buildings across the river. Incredibly, given our previous warnings about pictures of rivers, city overlooks and military sites, the guide said, "This is a great place to take pictures!" He, our silent Russian escorts, and the driver then left the bus, walked around the front end, and stood with their backs to us and the scenery. I wondered, "Is this a trap? Are we being set up?" Except for my sleeping friend, the rest of the group disembarked to click away; Patricia and I joined them. I decided this was one of those situations in life where it would be easier to obtain forgiveness than permission. The behavior of our escorts reminded me of Sergeant Shultz in the television situation comedy *Hogan's Heroes*: "I see nothing!" Enjoying the scenery with us were formally dressed grooms with their brides. Apparently, many Moscow couples are allowed to take their wedding day off from work to celebrate with a trip to the Hills. This reminded me of Niagara Falls.

That evening, we were pleasantly surprised by being given the option to attend the Moscow Circus, which was not on our original schedule. Of course, we wanted to take advantage of this once in a lifetime opportunity! We went deep beneath the surface of the city on giant escalators to reach the Moscow subway, which ran through miles of tunnels blasted into solid rock, taking us to the circus grounds. The talented clowns did not need language to perform successfully. The acrobats in aerial demonstrations did what I thought were impossible feats. The Cossacks demonstrated their horsemanship and skill with the cutlass and saber. A dozen of them were riding around the ring at full gallop chopping off the tops of wooden posts as they went past. Suddenly, a commanding shout was heard! Without slackening pace, every rider threw his sword high in a twirling arc. Every weapon was caught by the handle by another rider, none were missed! I still don't believe it!

My inquisitive nature almost got me into serious trouble one night in Moscow. I thought someone with my expertise in electronics could find a listening bug if there was one. Combing over the room, I found what looked like a small radio behind the planter. It was plugged into a wall convenience outlet. Since it looked like the only candidate for my search; and since we had no intention of trying to listen to a Russian language broadcast, I unplugged it. As we were leaving the room in the morning, a large, excited Russian matron confronted me at the door. She was shaking her head and her finger, first pointing at me and then in the direction of the planter. I didn't understand anything, but I suddenly remembered the value of the Berry College pens in my pocket. I quickly took one out, still wrapped in clear cellophane, and held it up. She stopped motioning, peered at the pen, grabbed it, and quickly disappeared. I heaved a sigh of relief and did not look for any more bugs.

We spent the better part of that beautiful Sunday visiting the tourist attractions associated with Red Square, a large paved rectangle long enough to use as a runway for small planes and over one-half a mile wide. At the south end of the Square, St. Basil's Cathedral was remarkable for its very colorful towers and domes. The famous GUM Department Store lined one side of the Square, while Lenin's tomb and the public access to the Kremlin were on the opposite side. Located off one corner of the Square, the Church of the Twelve Apostles and the Patriarch's Palace were the headquarters of what is left of the traditional Russian Orthodox Church allowed to function under the Communist government. As we arrived, long lines of people were waiting to visit the churches and Lenin's Tomb. Our guide emphasized the artistic value of the preserved icons at the basement level of the Patriarch's Palace. As we walked around the tombs of the Patriarchs at that level, we viewed the icons, which were organized like a pictorial Bible depicting events from Genesis forward. There was a throng of people working their way through, but as in St. Isaac's Cathedral, I sensed that we were the only tourists there. The thought occurred to me that maybe this was the only Bible these people were allowed to read.

The Kremlin was a large, long, red brick structure beside the Volga River. Not being allowed into the more secret nooks and crannies, we toured the civilian government parts of the building. Inside the Kremlin was an auditorium with thousands of seats, each featuring special audio connections to the stage and to booths where interpreters worked. The meetings of the World Congress of Communism were held here, hence the occasional need for foreign interpreters. We went back to this auditorium in the evening to watch the very colorful opera, *Madam Butterfly,* performed in Italian. Of course, we did not understand the lyrics, but good music does not need words to be appreciated. The opera conveyed very clearly by action and costume that the villain of the story was an American naval officer.

The next day, those of us having no desire to view Lenin under glass obtained permission to leave the group and tour the GUM Department Store. Its booths were similar in structure and operation to the department store in Leningrad, except there were multiple levels, with much nicer architecture finishing, and service available to foreigners. Prices were very competitive for the American dollar, but we only picked up small souvenirs.

Before leaving Moscow, we toured more vocational schools. We were also taken to shop at a special store which only served foreigners. This facility was setup architecturally and operationally like Sears or Macy's stores here in America. There was a big section devoted to fur products from Siberia, with very attractive prices. However, there would not be much opportunity to wear such clothing in Georgia. We did purchase a few things.

We flew out of Moscow headed for Munich, Germany, by way of Vienna, Austria. I have never understood the necessity for such serious security; but as we came down the plane's exit steps in Vienna, we were greeted by soldiers on each side with automatic assault rifles raised on alert. Nothing was said to explain their presence. I have always wondered if they met every flight from Russia in that manner. In spite of our greeting party, Patricia and I had an irrational feeling of relief at no longer being under the control of the Soviets. We changed planes and went on to Munich, Germany.

Germany

Our tour of Munich was highlighted by time spent in the Deutsches Musem, which was fully as interesting as a visit to our own Smithsonian Institution. The exhibit featuring the development of printing started with Johann Gutenberg's press and Bible. The history of the piano and other musical instruments was well-told with many preserved examples. Later in the week, Patricia and I were able to spend another couple of hours there.

After a two-hour bus ride on the Autobahn, we visited the Castle of King Lugwig II, 1845-1886. The Neuschwanstein Castle is in the Bavarian Alps, near the Austrian border. The territory reminded us of the scenery in the *Sound of Music,* and the exterior of the Castle was the inspiration for the enchanted castle that Walt Disney's Tinkerbelle Fairy flies around.

There were the usual lectures on education in Germany, and we toured an apprentice training school. By this time, most of us were too saturated with information about the various European educational systems to appreciate one more round. The young interpreter did not help our mood. He was an American student, studying somewhere in England, who had landed a summer job, obviously beyond his competencies. He would listen intently to the German educators, nodding his head in apparent agreement, saying "Yeah, Yeah." My personal competence in the German language is non-existent, but from listening to Sergeant Schultz, I think he was trying to mean, "Yes, Yes." When one of us would clear his or her throat, he would suddenly realize he was not participating in a private conversation, turn to us, and too often say, "There is no good translation of that into English." For the sake of pleasant goodwill, we pretended he had translated satisfactorily to us, nodded our heads, and tried to look interested.

Going Home

    The time to return home had come. We boxed up literature we had collected with non-fragile souvenirs and shipped them home. We flew to London, changed planes, and continued to New York. My sister, Rita, with her family, still living on Long Island, gave us a surprise welcome at the JFK Airport. We had time enough to enjoy a snack supper with them before our flight to Syracuse. By midnight, Patricia's parents with Chip and Richard had met us in Syracuse and taken us to Fabius. I felt good to be near home with my family intact again.

    The Goodwill Mission had been an opportunity and experience of a lifetime. Although delegates from America had been given little opportunity to provide information about our programs, I did learn a lot about vocational education in the countries we visited. My professional resume had been greatly enhanced. Little did I suspect that the Unseen Hand had been preparing me for an equally great leadership opportunity in the future.

Chapter 21

Building a Long Term Home

Upon my return from the Goodwill Mission, I was able to spend my free time during the rest of the summer resuming our goal of moving the family into a home of our own. Berry's rent was very reasonable, but the experiences of a couple of long-term employees made me aware of a financial downside. Upon retirement, they had to move off campus and find private housing without equity in a home. I determined not to fall into that trap.

I had purchased a high and dry virgin lot which the whole family had started clearing of brush, brambles, and smaller pine trees in preparation for building. Patricia and Richard found out the hard way that they were very sensitive to poison ivy and oak. We then obtained a building permit from the County Building Department. When the Goodwill Tour materialized, we changed our plans. I visited a local dealer in modular manufactured homes. For a reasonable cost, he would move the two halves of a manufactured home onto a concrete foundation, providing a full three-bedroom home with two baths which would meet all requirements of the Southern Building Code for permanent structures. I would only need to build an attached garage and game room to have all the functions we desired. I signed the contract and arranged the mortgage before leaving for Europe. Once we were settled, I felt like a pioneer clearing land for my garden, grape arbor, and fruit trees as a spare time hobby. I acquired two large iron water tanks to save rainwater for irrigation. I bought a used multipurpose garden tractor to mow grass and break up the soil. Much later, we purchased the adjacent lot expanding my farm to more than one acre. Patricia worked hard making this lot a well landscaped addition to our homestead. The place required a lot of maintenance work from all of us, but it was a comfortable fit for a family with our roots. We lived at 32 Johns Drive for twenty-four years.

By the year 2000, our age and health issues dictated a much lower maintenance level and relaxed lifestyle. We sold the Johns Drive property and purchased a home more suited to future retirement in North Woods, a newer subdivision, where we still reside in 2013.

Chapter 22

Promotion and Tenure

Of course, building and settling our nest could not be our only concern at this point in my academic career. Achieving promotion to full professor and being awarded full tenure rights are major milestones in a college professor's life requiring years of hard work and preparation. To achieve these long-term goals, I had to be able to show a continued pattern of growth in teaching excellence, academic achievement, and commendable service. I needed to be able to show that I was a professional author. Like so many significant needs in my life, the solution to this one came by a surprise phone call.

Becoming a Published Author

Mr. Loper, my mentor from Oswego State College who had retired to Florida, called to request that I ghost write a new chapter on solid state electronics for a basic electricity textbook which he and another co-author had been marketing through Delmar Publishers of Albany, NY. When he forwarded my new chapter to Delmar Publishers, the technical editor demanded to know who had really written that material. Mr. Loper confessed that I had been hired to help him. The editor was not happy; he wanted all legal understandings described, and notarized.

Delmar Publishers flew me to Albany for an evaluative review of my qualifications and a personal interview. When the dust settled, I had a contract to make a thorough revision of the book and generate an accompanying laboratory manual. In compensation, the publishers would list me as a co-author, sharing the royalties from future sales. Ultimately the book was published under two titles:

(1) *Introduction to Electricity and Electronics*, Third Edition, by Loper, Ahr, and Clendenning, published by Delmar, 1978, which was for the American school market.
(2) *Basic Electricity and Electronics*, Third Edition, by Loper, Ahr, and Clendenning, published by Van Nostrand Reinhold, 1978, which was for international markets.

The books were used in a significant number of high schools and technical colleges. After ensuring a rigorous education at Oswego, Mr. Loper had now been instrumental in boosting my recognition in the technical education community. I have learned from Mr. Loper's example and personal experience that the success of my students is the greatest personal reward a teacher can realize. Five of my students were State or National Industrial Arts Teachers of the Year.

Achieving Promotion and Tenure

My dossier of achievements met any reasonable standards for promotion and tenure. I had excellent student evaluations, and I had revised all curricula offered by the Department. My professional service resume had grown as Patricia and I worked on growing the Department, sharing innovations, and serving the related professional organizations. We had raised over $30,000 for an endowed scholarship in honor of Dr. James Luton, the immediate past Department Head. The European Goodwill Tour and following presentations supported the necessary professional recognition. Becoming a published author capped my academic production section of the dossier. My only concern regarding the promotion and tenure evaluation was that my strong actions in campus politics might be held against me in the anonymous deliberations of the Promotion and Tenure Advisory Committee. Campus politics was still in turmoil as some faculty were trying to get the students involved in complaints against the administration. My concerns were allayed when the Trustees announced my promotion and tenure.

Post-Tenure Activities

I realized that I was still in the relatively early years of my academic career, and I could not afford to rest on my laurels and coast to retirement. I was challenged by the potential of my present position to make positive contributions to my students and my profession. The State-funded summer workshops put me in contact with the best teachers and leaders in such professional organizations as the Georgia Industrial Arts Association, the Georgia Vocational Association, the Georgia Association of Educators, and the Southeastern Industrial Arts Association. I participated in the national associations affiliated with each of the state professional groups. Often in our travels, Patricia and I could squeeze in a partial day of sightseeing with the boys at local areas of interest, such as the St. Louis Arch and President Lincoln's tomb. I collaborated with officers and committees of these organizations to improve service to their members, lobbied for funding, established new curriculum guides, and evaluated and revised teacher certification standards and tests. I really had little interest in seeking elective offices, but did fulfill a few.

Patricia and I enjoyed hosting association conferences on campus, usually including campus tours and a banquet because such gatherings not only allowed us to fellowship with others sharing our professional goals, but also exposed outsiders to the Berry campus, history, and mission. I started serving a number of three year terms on the Editorial Board of *Man, Society, and Technology*, the professional journal of the American Industrial Arts Association.

As President-elect of the Georgia Vocational Association, I was responsible for the main programs for the 1982 Summer Conference held annually in Atlanta, GA. At our final meeting, the Association sponsored a major debate among the three candidates for Governor in the up-coming election. We were fortunate to obtain the services of the popular Atlanta TV news anchor, Monica Kaufman, to monitor the debate. (Now, over thirty years later, Monica is still on the air nightly, but she uses her married name, Monica Pearson.) The debate and election was won by the Honorable Jo Frank Harris, who served two terms as Governor. Sponsoring the debate made him more aware of vocational education programs in the state, and he was a strong supporter of our programs throughout his terms.

Maintaining evolving high standards for industrial technology students was as challenging as the teacher education programs. To help maintain standards, I started serving on the Accreditation Committee of the National Association of Industrial Technology. At first, I was a Visiting Team Member, but I progressed to being the Visiting Team Chair, responsible for scheduling the visitations, assigning team members to areas of inspection, and assembling and editing the final reports. As a Committee, we were able to help correct weaknesses in a number of programs from the Northeast to the Midwest.

In time, I also became an Editorial Referee for the *Journal of Industrial Technology*, the official publication of the Association. We followed procedures for blind peer review of articles submitted by professionals in the field. I played the role of constructive critic more than referee, attempting to make redeeming suggestions, knowing that some young professor's career might depend on the ultimate publication of his or her work. Waiting for a report of the Editorial Board was an anxious time for me when I had to send my own work through the same review process. I continued this editorial service until my heart by-pass operation in the fall of 2007.

Chapter 23

Fun with Family
"All work and no play makes Jack a dull boy."

We did have a lot of fun as Chip and Richard were growing. They attended middle school and high school at Berry Academy, which was then a residential school on the Mountain Campus (now Winshape Center and Berry Elementary School). Children of Berry employees and a few local families commutated each day. The boys were both excellent soccer and basketball players, and we managed to arrange many of our professional and service activities around their games. At home games, while the female teams played first, we would sell candy, popcorn, and hotdogs, and then relinquish the refreshment booth to other parents while the boys played. I could often arrange a recruiting trip or evaluation visit to a State workshop participant in or near the community of their away games.

"Ship of Fools"

The Oostanaula River flowing through Floyd County and Rome provided the opportunity for canoe trips and a couple of home built raft races sponsored by the Rome-Floyd County Recreation Authority. Prizes were to be awarded for the fastest trip and the most unusual raft.

We had plenty of lumber for a Huckleberry Finn type of raft, but I thought that would not be unusual enough.

Talking about the first contest with my neighbor Ron Taylor, I casually remarked that maybe empty milk jugs might be used as floatation devices. Within two days, I came home from Berry to find a truckload of empty milk jugs dumped on my lawn. Ron had obtained the jugs through a supplier to his parents' small grocery store. He and his young son, Mike, wanted to join us in whatever adventure we devised.

To make three, usable, flotation pontoons, the boys and I lined up crates of jugs along the lengths of wide flat boards. A matching board was laid over the tops of the crates to walk on and keep the jugs from escaping upward as they tended to float. We used wire to wrap around the pontoons, holding the boards and crates in place. We separated the three pontoons and held them in place by three cross boards bolted to the boards on top of the crates. The result was a jug supported raft which would float five people—very unusual we thought!

Ron had a friend with an artistic interest who drew a cartoon style poster depicting the raft and the crew. The artist captured Ron's Blackbeard whiskers, Chip's big glasses, and my balding head. He put a banner over the raft carrying the caption, "SHIP of FOOLS." That seemed to characterize our jovial spirit. I silk-screened the image on tee shirts for the crew.

The raft supported us very well, but the crates created a lot of drag as we tried to paddle it through the water. It took us hours longer to complete the course than we had anticipated. By the time we floated past the Judges' Stand in downtown Rome, the judges had all gone home, having awarded the most unusual prize to a Huckleberry Finn type of craft. The boys had worked very hard, but we were not too disappointed because we had lots of fun. We knew in our hearts that we were winners!

The following year I came up with another unusual design for the river raft race using empty, fifty-five gallon barrels. Paddles were attached to two of the barrels which were powered by someone with good balance walking on a third one, forcing it to turn. This system was inspired by watching loggers in a burling contest on television. We didn't win that year either. We did not get a third try at the race because the Athletic Association stopped sponsoring the event. I think if the competitions had continued, we would have eventually had a winning entry.

Encouraging Work Experiences

We wanted our sons to have some employment experience beyond doing yard work at home. Berry's tradition of providing work for both Academy and college students helped provide such experiences. One summer, Chip worked on the grounds crew, mostly caring for the gardens at the House of Dreams at the top of Lavender Mountain. The House of Dreams was a cool, rustic retreat built for Martha Berry in the days when there was no air conditioning on the campus. She allowed her students to use it as a honeymoon suite. Since Chip was too young to drive, Patricia had to take him to work and pick him up. Quite often at the end of a work day, Chip would meet her at the base of the mountain because he had learned that he could run down the mountain on a well-used path quicker than she could drive up the winding dirt road.

Richard also participated in the Berry work experience program on the janitorial cleaning crew. He cleaned windows and carpets in many of the buildings on both the College and the Academy campuses. Having access to the President's Office to clean the carpet intrigued him. Both boys worked in turn picking up trash on the Mountain Campus Road.

The summer before Chip went away to college, he obtained a job in the kitchen of Floyd Medical Center running a commercial dishwasher. It was hot, heavy work. He also pushed the food carts to and from patients' rooms. By school time, he was thoroughly convinced that he needed an education to make his living some other way. Later, Richard also worked for the hospital, rolling the food carts to serve the patients in their rooms and picking up the used trays.

Patricia and I felt blessed and proud to have such well-rounded sons, each with a grounded faith, caring heart, and good work ethic. Both boys were valedictorians in their turn. Chip spent three semesters studying electrical engineering at Washington University in St. Louis, MO, before transferring to the Georgia Institute of Technology in Atlanta (Georgia Tech). Richard went to Georgia Tech directly out of high school. Both of our sons tutored others and taught undergraduate classes for Tech during their graduate work. Richard called his basic electricity teaching assignment for athletes, "Shocks for Jocks." Both boys received Bachelors and Masters Degrees in Electrical Engineering with highest honors from Tech. As hard as they worked, there was still enough fun along the way to keep them from becoming "dull boys."

Patricia's Fun—Bowling

Right after our move to Rome, Patricia joined Monday night and Wednesday morning woman's bowling leagues. The next year, she was elected secretary to both leagues which she enjoyed because the positions were very compatible with her bookkeeping background. Keeping the leagues records also paid enough to cover her bowling fees. When we purchased our first personal computer system, Richard wrote a spreadsheet program to keep the records and prepare the reports for her. The experience provided some family togetherness each week. Eventually, the bowling alley set up their own computerized league record system, but there were so many bugs that Patricia was correcting its output against hers almost weekly. She was always right. After the boys left home, Patricia and I had a standing appointment on Monday evenings as I helped her administer the leagues and cheer on her team.

Patricia and I enjoyed going to her bowling tournaments out of town. One time, all of her team members, with their spouses, happened to arrive at the same time in the parking lot of the Heart of Dixie Motel in Birmingham, Alabama. We all trouped into the lobby, single file, and turned to face the front desk. The clerk had his attention diverted until finally looking up to see the line of eight people. Not knowing who to serve next, he thought if he said anything, one of us would probably request service. As he scanned us from his right to the left, he said, "Do **you'all** want a regular or a king bed?" Patricia and I both lost it. We could picture all eight of us trying to share a regular bed! The others, all true blue Southerners, thought we were crazy. They hadn't heard anything funny at all. That made the situation even funnier. Finally, I guess they concluded that all Yankees were weird, and somebody stepped forward to book a room.

Chapter 24

Leading a Vocational Education Delegation on a Chinese Scientific Exchange

I will never know how my work came to the attention of people in higher places. It is part of the mystery of the workings of the Unseen Hand. In August of 1984, I received a letter from Dr. Robert Everett, Executive Director of China-US Scientific Exchanges, asking if I would be willing to assemble and lead a delegation of American Vocational Educators on an exchange tour of schools in the People's Republic of China during the summer of 1985. China-US Scientific Exchanges was identified as a non-profit foundation approved by both the US and Chinese governments to facilitate scientific and cultural exchanges between professionals in both nations. Dr. Everett assured me that personnel at the Exchanges Foundation would assist me in suggesting a travel itinerary and identification of Chinese schools and counterparts to visit. In October, I received the official invitation from the International Exchange Service of the China Association for Science and Technology in Beijing, China. When I shared the invitation letter with Berry's administration, they were supportive, so I agreed to accept the responsibility.

Lee R. Clendenning, PhD

Patricia completes a "Fearless Flying" course

I was determined not to go to China without Patricia, who was so fearful of flying that she had come home from Europe a basket case, determined never to fly again. I discussed the problem with a local travel agent who suggested a "Fearless Flying" course designed for people like her, and sponsored by Emory University in cooperation with Delta Airlines. I enrolled us both, and plopped the admission papers on the desk in front of her, begging her to at least attend the first session. She finally agreed to go to the first class, but made no commitment for the future. We completed the course, one night at a time.

The Fearless Flying course was money well spent. Professional stewardesses explained all procedures, strange noises, and causes of turbulence. A psychologist provided stress-relieving techniques. Experts in weather and navigation explained how the company kept track of the location of planes and how storms were predicted and avoided. We were taken on a field trip to the Atlanta control tower to watch the flight controllers communicating with pilots as they taxied, landed, and took off. Chip and Richard joined us on another field trip to the demonstration of a flight simulator. Internally, the simulator was so realistic that when the pilot decided it was time to take off, poor Patricia panicked and tried to leave. The pilot finally convinced her that we really would not fly anywhere from inside the enclosed warehouse! Seriously, the images projected on the windows, the sound of the engines, and the motions of the craft were unbelievably realistic. We took off in good weather, flew around downtown Atlanta, and landed safely again. We did it again at night, and one more time during a terrible rainstorm. The pilot let Chip try his hand at the controls. It was a grand evening.

The graduating experience for the class was a real flight from Atlanta to Orlando, Florida, for an overnight visit to Disney World. For some mysterious, undiagnosed reason at the time, Patricia had developed swollen feet, ankles, and legs, making walking very painful. Delta allowed Chip and Richard to join us. They pushed their mother around to the various exhibits and shows in a wheel chair. Handicapped people and their parties were always ushered to the front of the long lines and into the best seating areas. The boys decided if they ever returned, they would come back with a handicapped friend! There was a culminating party and a return flight, everything at Delta's expense. On the way back, a stewardess was assigned to Patricia to explain things and ease her fears. I assured Patricia that I didn't expect her ever to like flying. But, I needed her help on the China tour. Like the trooper she has always been, she agreed to go.

Recruiting a delegation

The rest of the fall of 1984 and early winter of 1985 was spent recruiting other members of the delegation. I checked professional directories for association officers, professors and administrators in colleges and universities that had vocational teacher education programs. In all, Patricia and I sent out 380 letters of announcement with invitations, detailed expectations, and application procedures. I am sure the number of applicants was greatly limited by the fact that I did not have a budget. All applicants were expected to solicit funds for themselves and a possible companion from their own institutions or pay the costs themselves. Many had questions about details of travel and living conditions within China which I could not provide, down to which schools and industries we would visit and the availability of modern toilets. By agreements between our two countries, the Bamboo Curtain that had hidden most details about China had been lifted for exchanges such as mine only four years previously. My delegates would have to have an adventurous spirit and flexibility enough to make the best of whatever we found.

Each delegate needed to submit a resume and draft or outline of the topic he or she would share at meetings with Chinese counterparts. Those documents had to be approved by the Chinese before an official invitation was extended. When the roster was complete, there were a total of eighteen of us (counting spouses and traveling companions) representing many regions of the country, different curricular divisions, and different levels of vocational-technical education.

Lee R. Clendenning, PhD

China, here we come!

The personnel at China-US Scientific Exchanges kept their promise to assist in all aspects of the tour. By March 12, 1985, I was able to send a letter to all delegates with firm departure details, a tentative list of cities to be visited, the resumes of all participants, and the outlines or drafts of all topics to be presented. The Exchanges assisted with the applications for visas, made all reservations for airline, land travel, and lodging, and planned a general orientation conference in San Francisco, California, prior to embarking. Through the China Association of Science and Technology, they arranged all the school visitations, industrial tours, and professional meetings. Their Executive Director, Dr. Robert Everett, did not travel with us, but he was in China during our visit and worked out problems in our itinerary as the visit progressed.

Many of the party, including myself, wanted to use 35 mm. slides or an overhead projector during their presentation. To operate properly, this equipment required a stable source of electrical power. I learned that commercial power in China varied greatly in voltage and connection type from location to location. Remembering the old Chinese proverb, "One picture is worth a thousand words;" I assured my delegates that I would make provisions to use their modern audio-visuals. I then designed and built a heavy duty transformer which I could connect to whatever power the Chinese had, and adjust the output to the American standard. I also purchased a pocket-sized voltmeter. The transformer and audio-visual equipment added to our luggage count and travel weight, but proved to be very valuable in achieving our success.

Since six members of the touring party were from Georgia, we travelled together to the formal gathering point in San Francisco via Minneapolis, Minnesota. The Georgia contingent included Mrs. Ellen Coody, the Executive Secretary to the Georgia Vocational Association, with her husband Jim, Dr. Ouida Dickey, Associate Dean of Berry College, and her sister-in law traveling companion Faye Dickey, and, of course, Patricia and me. In addition to being one of my administrators and a personal friend, Dr. Dickey was a state and national leader in business and economic education. The weather was clear as we flew, so I was able to look down on the Dakota Badlands and immediately understood their name because they looked like they could not support life any better than the surface of the moon. I also reasoned that the Flats of the Great Salt Lakes were also rightly named, since we could have easily landed our 747 there. The western mountains were beautiful, and the weather was nice as we landed in San Francisco.

We were fortunate that Ellen Coody was very familiar with San Francisco. She rented a car and gave the Georgia group a whirlwind tour of the city. Going down the hilly curves of Lodi Street with her was as thrilling as any amusement ride I had ever experienced. She ducked around the streetcars and took us out to Candlestick Baseball Park and over the Golden Gate Bridge. We had dinner at The Fisherman's Wharf.

Since our China orientation was scheduled at a dinner meeting the following evening, we had time in the morning to share with Patricia's sister, Evelyn, and her family. Evelyn's husband, Tyler, was the pastor of a church in Willows, California. They met us for breakfast and a trip to the Embarcadero Waterfront. We could look across the water at the abandoned Alcatraz Prison. After lunch, we returned to the hotel, and prepared to meet the rest of my delegation.

Mrs. Robert Everett, wife of the Exchange Director, briefed us on protocol for formal dinners in China. There would be the expectation of multiple toasts expressing the pleasure of being there, expressions of good will, and a desire to maintain contacts and friendships. When introduced to an individual, one was to bow at the same time the new acquaintance did; otherwise, the Chinese were determined to bow last. All meals would have multiple courses, and in spite of what one may have been told by his or her mother, we were not to clean our plates completely between courses. If one course was completely devoured, they would bring some more of the same. We were not to use American currency except at official exchange locations.

We left San Francisco at noon Pacific Time on Sunday, June 24, 1985, for Tokyo, Japan. When asked how long the flight would be, the stewardess replied, "Three meals and two movies." The flight was uneventful. The flight from Tokyo to Hong Kong was well under way when the pilot's voice came over the intercom with an old joke:

"The good news is that we have favorable winds and are making good time. The bad news is that we don't know where we are going."

Only this time he was serious! He explained that Hong Kong was being hit by a category three typhoon, and he was waiting for a decision whether to detour to Taipei, Taiwan, or continue on the scheduled route. A while later, he reported that we were past the point of possible detours, and we would continue to Hong Kong. The runway at Hong Kong is built like a narrow earth-filled pier which reaches out into the water of the harbor. Fighting the poor visibility of blinding rain and the cross winds of the storm, the pilot landed on this hazardous strip. There were no atheists on board by that time!

Representatives from China-US Scientific Exchanges were there to greet us with a big sign: "Welcome to Hong Kong, Clendenning Delegation." The Exchange people had booked us into a first rate hotel across the street from the airport terminal. In our room, there was a second welcome sign, a big basket of fresh fruit including melons, grapes, apples, and oranges, and a refrigerator with different drinks. We had been provided the nicest accommodations we had ever experienced. We hadn't seen a bed in over forty hours.

The storm was still raging in the morning as we went to a breakfast buffet. Looking out the hotel window, I could see the airport runway disappear into rain and fog. Our flight was rescheduled for noon. We were approved by Customs as the storm cleared, and were off to Beijing, China, in another American-made 747 with a friendly all Chinese crew. At lunch, we were issued silverware, but Chinese travelers were given chopsticks. As we flew, we filled out the papers for declarations of how much currency, jewelry, and electronic equipment we were taking into China. As was the case with my Russian visit, everything would have to be accounted for when we left the country.

Beijing

Beijing was warm and sunny as we were met by the very personable and articulate Mr. Qiang Sui, our guide and interpreter for the duration of the entire China tour. He was an English instructor for Beijing University assigned to us as a summer job. He had a female assistant who also traveled with us. An engineering student, she was very pleasant, but struggled some with English translations. While we were in the Beijing area, we were also assigned a small, but very modern tour bus with a regular driver. The bus had a PA system for tour narrations.

The hour-long bus ride to the Friendship Hotel gave us our first impression of China. Although there were a few automobiles and some horse-drawn wagons, human muscle power appeared to be one of the prime movers on the highway. Hundreds of bicycles were all obeying the same traffic signals and sharing the same pavement as our bus. Some bicycles were towing carts loaded with goods apparently headed to or from markets. Others had make-shift racks which helped balance loads piled high. I saw six men harnessed to a long steel bridge beam balanced on a two wheeled axle. I wondered how far they had to move it. Some two-wheeled carts were balanced as they were pushed from behind. There were also many rickshaw type carts pulled from the front. A few heavier trucks appeared to be military vehicles converted to civilian use. Many "tractor trailers" were really what looked like our single cylinder, two-wheeled garden tractors hitched in a unique way to a two-wheeled trailer. Each unit of the pair balanced its mate while allowing the driver to sit on the trailer load steering the tractor by handle forks. These vehicles were carrying what appeared to be about three wheelbarrow loads of heavy brick, rock, or stony gravel. I could not help but think that people with this kind of ingenuity and willingness to work would someday be a world power with which to be reckoned.

Our destination, the Friendship Hotel, was a former college campus with pleasant, shaded walkways among the buildings, which had been modified for use by exchange groups such as ours. We were assigned rooms in a multi-story dorm and served meals in a large group dining room on round tables, decorated with fresh flowers. We were allowed silverware for breakfast, but told we must master chopsticks for our other meals. For soups, there were small spoon-like ladles, manufactured as hand-decorated, fine china. When we complemented the staff on the evening meal through our interpreter, we received the reply, "It does not matter."

When we retired to our room, I saw a large thermos bottle filled with steaming water. Because we had been warned not to drink any water without boiling, I checked with Mr. Sui and learned that all rooms would be supplied with boiled water in case we wanted to make a cup of tea or some broth. He took me to the building boiler room where the hot water was tapped off from the building's furnace. This process was interesting and very thoughtful of our hosts. He informed me that bottled soft drinks were made from boiled water, but their ice cream was made with unpasteurized milk.

The Jing-Song Vocational School in the suburbs of Beijing was the first that we visited. We had an initial meeting with the school President and several teachers around a big conference table with Mr. Sui interpreting. Afterwards, we were allowed to tour the classrooms and laboratories freely. We were surprised to learn that many skilled trade vocational programs had actual production quotas where the products of their laboratory practice were delivered into the government-run economy, providing practical, real world experience.

Tian'anmen Square and the Forbidden City

In the afternoon, we visited Tian'anmen Square and the adjacent Forbidden City. Like Red Square in Moscow, Tian'anmen Square was a paved area large enough to land a small plane in either direction. There were families flying beautiful, multi-colored kites of all shapes and sizes. A flying dragon seemed the most popular. At one end of the Square, a Chinese movie production regarding some historical event was under way. There were lots of medieval looking soldiers and other people in period costumes going through their action scenes. There was no hint of the future troubles that would capture world attention to the Square.

The Chinese were very proud of the fact that they could now enter the forbidden, walled city where once only the ruling families lived. Over a moat bridge and inside the windowless brick exterior, we were taken to the buildings which were the center of government in past dynasties. We saw where the virgins were housed and where the servant eunuchs had to live. We could not read the signs and captions on wall posters, but it was obvious that our narrators much preferred the Communist ideals of their present form of government over what they had been taught about life under the old system.

Our first formal dinner meeting with the officers of the China Association of Science and Technology went well. We were individually introduced through interpreters, and during the first set of toasts, the Association President welcomed us and assured us that they were pleased to show us their schools and industries. I responded, expressing our happiness for having the opportunity to meet them and describing what I assumed to be our common commitment to the vocational education of the youth of our countries. There were smiles and nods all around. Talking through an interpreter on this occasion, and others as the tour progressed, gave me time to gather my thoughts between sentences. Usually, the interpretation took about as much time as my presentation. However, a few times after one of my longer sentences, the interpreter would say only a few, short words and look back for my next thought. At those times, I was sure his Chinese interpretation to the audience was, "I haven't a clue!" Sharing a spirit of good will is easy when one is talking to the most polite people in the world.

After breakfast the next day, we were off to see Panda bears at the Beijing Zoo. Rather than turn us loose at the entrance, the small tour bus followed the paved footpaths around the other buildings right up to the Panda cages, where we left the bus and started taking pictures. There were big, classical Pandas, baby Pandas, and smaller multi-colored Pandas up in the tree branches eating leaves.

We toured Beijing University by following the walkways around the University campus as Mr. Sui narrated. At the main administration building, and a few of the other buildings, the bus stopped for us to take pictures from the opened windows. We were not allowed to leave the bus to interview students.

We were allowed to leave the bus and walk half way around the perimeter of a beautiful lake at the Summer Palace where we saw classical Chinese scenery with arched bridges over streams, colorful covered walkways, and flowering lotus plants on the water. The Palace had the curved pagoda-style, tile roof which was supported by multi-colored columns. Young women in pretty traditional Chinese costumes graced the entryways. The personal Theater of the Emperor featured multiple stages for scene changes, but seating for an audience of one!

By this time of the day, Mother Nature was calling pretty hard. We had our first introduction to Eastern-style toilets. The men's room provided a rain gutter nailed to the wall at about knee height, tilted to drain out of the building at one end. There were also two holes in the floor about five inches in diameter, with a water hose coiled on the wall and connected to a controlling facet. The women reported only the target holes in the floor and the water hose. We had been warned in San Francisco to carry lots of Kleenex with us. Except for fine restaurants and hotels, these accommodations were typical, even in the schools.

We ate a late lunch consisting of multiple courses of lotus. First there were the bulbs, prepared like an onion soup. Then lotus stems were served as we would serve asparagus; they were kind of tough. The lotus leaves and blossoms were presented as we would serve leaf spinach. It was a unique meal, but we were all ready for dinner that evening.

Dinner was at the Five Dragon Restaurant which was on the shore of the lake we had walked around. The food was good, but nothing like the Chinese food served here. Fresh and cooked vegetables, rice soup, fish, and chicken were presented in large dishes on a lazy Susan in the center of the table. Diners turned the server to access the dishes desired. We struggled with the chopsticks. Again, when we complemented the staff, they answered, "It does not matter."

Back at the hotel that Friday evening, I asked Mr. Sui if Patricia and I could attend a Christian Church on Sunday. He promptly replied that there were no Christian churches in Beijing. When shown from our guide book that a Christian Church was serving the European diplomatic community in the Chinese capital, he then said he would look into the matter. On Saturday morning, he admitted that there was such a church, but the China Association of Science and Technology had no dealings with it; therefore, we could not be granted permission to attend the church. Since we were the guests of the Chinese, I made no further issue of the matter.

Epiphany at the Great Wall

On Saturday morning, we followed the Panda Bear Highway as we started the journey to the Great Wall. The modern four-lane, divided highway was named for the hundreds of painted Panda Bear silhouettes standing along both shoulders of the road. There were flowers blooming between the bears, a very impressive sight adding to our spirit of festivity. In the countryside, we passed large commune farms. There were family-sized gardens where we expected to see lawns. We were told that farm workers were allowed to grow vegetables in any of the small spaces around their homes for their immediate use, and any surplus could be sold at markets. That accounted for some of the loaded bicycle traffic we had observed. I was surprised to find this type of free enterprise existing with the blessing of the government. I noticed an apparent shortage of iron or mild steel because many buildings visible from the road had low pitched roofs with corrugated roofing held in place by heavy fieldstone rather than nails. I remarked to Mr. Sui that I didn't see any dogs around the farms. He looked at me kind of puzzled.

Finally, he said, "Dr. Clendenning, dogs are protein."

OK!

The terrain became more rugged as we approached some mountains. We passed stone and gravel quarries with more of the small tractor trailers moving the material. Going through some curved mountain passes, we parked on the side of the road with other tour vehicles. We were told that the Great Wall was a short walk ahead.

Hiking up the road following Mr. Sui, I looked higher to see my horizon defined by the silhouette of the Great Wall. A sudden wave of humility, gratitude, and personal fulfillment surged through me. I felt that only in the American land of opportunity in which I was raised, and only in stumbling in the light I had been given, and only with the help of many people doing the same thing, including my God-given soul mate, and only by the grace and providence of God's Unseen Hand orchestrating my life, could a poor, barefooted, seven-year-old boy, working the bean fields with migrant workers, become the leader of an International Delegation representing his chosen profession in China. I stopped still in my tracks, speechless!

"Lee, what is the matter?" Patricia asked.

I was too full of emotions to articulate any of them. After a moment, still gazing at the Wall, my only quiet response was, "I never thought I would ever see the Great Wall, much less walk on it!"

Seeing the Wall had never been a conscious goal of mine, no more than I had aspired to most of the other achievements in my life. The Wall triggered a realization of how much higher God's purposes had been for me than any aspirations of my own.

To one who had studied construction from my youth, the Great Wall represented an interesting project. It was placed on the watershed dividing ridge through the mountains so that no part of it would become a dam as rain drained off on both sides. However, this requirement meant that the structure curved and looped back on itself following the mountain ridges, requiring much more labor and material than following a surveyor's straight line path. Also, there was little excavation for the foundation rocks which also followed the lay of the land up and down the mountains rather than being placed level. Periodically, there were watch towers, built level and plumb, joining two sections of the Wall, with interior stone stairs connecting the ground and lookout levels. The top of the wall supported a narrow roadway lined by stone side shields.

We were allowed about an hour to explore in the area of the Great Wall. Patricia and I climbed to the top roadway and followed it about twenty minutes before returning to the ground level. There were vendors in small booths along the roadside. We purchased Tee-shirts with a nice silkscreened illustration of the Wall and the message, "I Walked on the Great Wall." Most of my party was late returning to the bus, and poor Mr. Sui was anxious to leave. Someone demanded of us, "What did you buy?" When we showed the shirts, the bus emptied because everyone had to have one. Mr. Sui expressed the thought that I, as a leader, should have more control of my people. I explained to him that a leader in our culture was most interested in meeting the needs of his people rather than having authority over them. This was a foreign concept to him. "If you are a leader, you are the boss!" he declared. I did not tell him that I had once seen a sign on a dean's desk that said, "Administering faculty is like herding cats!"

Other Sites of Interest

On another day, we enjoyed a pleasant bus ride through the countryside from Beijing to the Ming Tombs. To me, the most interesting aspects of this excursion was the lush fruit orchards on the rolling hills, and the way in which the Emperors of the Ming dynasty guarded the approach to the tomb campus. On both sides of the road, they placed large sculptured concrete statues of normally wild animals in pairs facing each other across the roadway, one standing guard while the other reclined in a restful position. The sight reminded me of the gathering of animals for Noah's ark. The elephants, tigers, and lions made great backdrops for individual and group photographs. Inside the brick-wall enclosed campus, the actual tombs were in a massive, multi-story building with lookout windows that provided an excellent view of the country.

Sunday morning, we visited the festive Children's Center. While the entrance sported a beautiful flower garden in full bloom, the inside was like an advanced McDonald's play area. Children appeared to be having fun tumbling on mats, bouncing on stretched canvas, and pedaling a trolley car around an overhead track following the perimeter of the building. Also, there were slides, and a running track. The building was well-lighted through ample window space and attractively decorated. The children were having healthy fun!

After the Children's Center, we visited the Temple of Heaven. This was a big round structure with two partial cone-shaped awning ring layers crowned by a full-cone dome and built on a high mound-shaped hill. The interior had many brightly colored columns, making decorative use of Chinese red! The complex was used by the Emperors of the Ming and Qing dynasties for annual ceremonies of prayer to Heaven for a good harvest.

Sunday afternoon, we were taken to a large department store where the bottom two floors were open to anyone and resembled the booth system we had seen in Russia. The upper two floors, allowing only foreigners, were set up more like American department stores with clerks behind glass-enclosed counters. In one area, they were selling the latest technology in cameras, electronic calculators, and other gadgets. American currency and credit cards were accepted.

Xian

We had to fly on a Chinese domestic airline to Xian (phonetically, "she-on"), the next city on our itinerary. As we approached the plane, a converted Russian bomber, I noticed the white inner cords showing through the worn down treads of the tires, which didn't do much for my confidence. The flight, already delayed two hours for what they called "flight repairs," took off, but it was soon dark and storming.

Later, in the turbulence, I could detect that we were descending. Down, down, down, we went while I could see nothing but rain beating on my window. Suddenly, the engines roared wide open, and we started to climb; we circled and repeated the descent followed by another roaring climb. After the third time, I was confident that the pilot was looking for the airport. I prayed, "Lord help him find it!" Eventually, following another long descent, there was a loud, jarring BANG! We ground to an emergency stop, still with nothing visible from my window. The Chinese stewardess, the male flight host, and Mr. Sui all kept straight stone faces. Orders were issued which Mr. Sui translated to mean, "Take your carry-on luggage and depart through the rear stairs," which had dropped down in place. Someone asked Mr. Sui if anything was wrong.

"No, nothing is wrong," he replied.

We all filed out into the rain, gathering under the shelter and light of the left wing. The flight host was talking to Mr. Sui while pointing into the distance. Following his indication, we could discern a pinpoint of light, maybe a mile away. There were no runway lights as one would expect at any other airport. Mr. Sui told us to walk toward the light, and we would find the terminal. I theorized that the poor lighting had made the landing strip difficult to find, and further, that one or more tires of the plane had blown out because of the hard landing. These suspicions were never confirmed. As we trudged toward the light in the rain, I silently thanked God for the lighthouse He was providing in the distance. I was worried about Patricia's state of mind, but she held up and never mentioned what her fears might have been. Her personal notes only recorded, "Bad flight!"

Terracotta Soldiers

The main tourist attraction near Xian was the excavation site of the Terracotta Soldiers that had been discovered in 1974 by a farmer plowing in the field. Apparently, Qin Shi Huang, the first Emperor of China, 200 years before Christ, had created an army of ceramic soldiers, their horses, chariots, and support personnel to guard his tomb after death. The army was buried with thick clay mud. A Swiss foundation funded a continuing exploration. By the time we visited in 1985, a large building had been built to shelter the site, and multiple rows of the standing army had been uncovered. We watched the workers removing the hard-caked mud, one spoonful at a time, so as not to damage the artifacts. According to a current Google search, estimates are that the pits containing the Terracotta Army hold over 8,000 soldiers, 130 chariots with 520 horses and 150 cavalry horses, the majority of which are still buried.

We also visited a large production factory and smaller industries in the Xian area. The large factory reminded me of our own mill and company towns during the last century. Workers lived in housing provided by the plant within walking distance of the jobs. Childcare was available on site and schools were nearby. A smaller ceramic plant was making colorfully glazed camels using slip casting for forming, and scrap wood for firing. The plant producing original cloisonné vases and other smaller vessels was also intriguing. Cloisonné workers were placing small pieces of colored metallic chips on the surface of flower vases, which were then kiln fired to create a beautiful enamel surface. These people were real artisans.

As our tour bus carried us around the city of Xian, we were able to get more insight into the life of common people. Women were doing their laundry using corrugated washboards in tubs on the sidewalk. There was more free enterprise than we expected. Barbers could be seen cutting men's hair. Tailors had pedal-powered sewing machines just outside their open shop doorways with bolts of silk, wool, and cotton standing on end leaning against their buildings. We were assured that they would be willing to measure us and produce a first class silk suit right on the spot. Housing was crowded and hot. In the evenings, men would squat outside of the buildings, chatting and smoking. Squatting low while balancing on the balls of their feet looked uncomfortable to us, but they seemed content in that position for extended periods of time.

An Opportunity to Teach in China Declined

In the hotel lobby, as we were waiting for the bus to take us to the train for our next journey, Mr. Sui asked me if I would be willing to come back to China for a two-year teaching appointment in one of their universities. Somewhat startled by the suggestion, I told him I would have to think about it and give him an answer later.

Amid all the honest good will and politeness which we had experienced, the obvious economic progress being made, and the inner desire to be helpful to such an industrious people, it would have been easy to forget some other realities, as many in the American intellectual community had done. What the Chinese touted as their progress had been purchased at a terrible price. The Chinese people still had a repressive Communist government. Population was being controlled by limiting families to only one child. Realistically, this goal could only be achieved by using abortion or infanticide when other birth control methods failed. Since families valued sons more than daughters, mothers were caught in the reverse situation of Jaochebed, the mother of Moses. I understand that through "agrarian reforms," thousands of their own people were stripped of their lands, murdered, or both. Thousands more were murdered or exiled in the government's effort to gain control and stifle political dissent. The only reason exchanges like mine were possible was that our government had caved to their demand that we give up a "Two Chinas" policy and recognize the People's Republic of China's right to eventually rule over anti-communist Taiwan.

As honored as I was by being offered a university position in China, after prayer and discussion with Patricia (who was against it), I decided to decline politely if the subject came up again. From all I was observing, my first reaction to the obvious energy and work ethic of the Chinese people was strengthened. I had predicted that, one day, China would represent a great economic and military challenge to the US. I did not want to hasten that day. I never considered the possibility of becoming an underground missionary as some are now doing. The offer was repeated a few days later, and I did decline without further explanation or future regrets. The events at Tian'anmen Square, in June of 1989, and our present world situation have confirmed to me that I had made the right decision.

Nanjing

Our next stop required an interesting twenty-three hour train ride from Xian to Nanjing. The train in which we were assigned sleeper cars, four bunks to a booth, appeared to be circa 1920. Some of the time, I stood in the car hallway looking out of the side windows which provided a much better view than the small window in the booth. Like all trains in any country, ours went through small communities and open fields. The large government-managed fields had elevated guard towers in the center, each manned by an armed soldier. Mr. Sui joined me.

"What are those?" I asked him, pointing to one of the towers.

"Those are guard towers."

"I thought you said there was no crime in China," I pressed.

"Well, the government places those in all big fields," he explained. I didn't press him further.

After a long silence, Mr. Sui asked, "What are you looking for?"

I decided to be honest and said, "Over the last century, European and American Christians sent quite a few missionaries to China. I am looking for any indication that they may have left of their presence; maybe small steeples on buildings, western—style tombstones, or crosses on anything from tombstones to buildings."

"You will not see anything;" Mr. Sui stated. "During the Cultural Revolution under Mao Zedong, all such symbols had to be taken down or destroyed."

I reluctantly gave up my search.

In Nanjing, the Chinese were very proud of a new double deck bridge across the Yangtze River. This river is the third largest in the world. Trains crossed the lower deck while auto, bicycle, and foot traffic went over the top. I was reminded of the Eads Bridge crossing our Mississippi River at St. Louis, Missouri. We were taken into the base of one of the bridge support towers on the River bank which also housed interesting exhibits describing the structural details and historical documentation of the progress of construction.

Our first meeting with educators in Nanjing was in school number fifty-one. We learned that there were fifty-nine numbered schools in the area. In the entrance to school number fifty-one, there was a big "Welcome to American Teachers" sign. The school was providing training in letterpress printing, mechanical drawing, metal machining, and auto mechanics. Other than the instructional posters in their language, their instructional facilities were much like our own.

Later, in a school teaching languages and business concepts necessary to establish trade with foreign markets, we were communicating through Mr. Sui's interpretation around a central table with teachers, administrators, local business leaders, and government officials. When Patricia decided to adjust the position of her chair without realizing that someone was standing close behind her, she bumped the gentleman gently. "I'm sorry," she automatically said. "That's OK," he said in very clear English. "You did not hurt me." As the conference ended, this gentleman disappeared. I wondered then how many other people did not need interpretation.

Another vocational school we visited had modern labs for computer-assisted drafting. In the parting conference, after two of my party had made their presentations, I was given a gift of two, machined hammer heads in a nice wooden presentation case. By then, I had heard many Chinese express gratitude with a two syllable expression which sounded to me like "she-she."

While accepting the gift, I said, "she-she." The room erupted in laughter. Puzzled, I said to Mr. Sui, "I wanted to say thank you. What did I say?"

"I will never tell you," he replied, with a smile still on his face. I still have the hammer heads.

For entertainment on the evening of July third, we were taken to a Chinese opera in a large community theater. The costumes were lovely, and the genuine native music interesting; however, we could not discern a story or narrative. The clown of my group (Isn't there one in every group?) started quietly telling his own story to fit the stage action. His story was humorous, but distracting. Most of my group was exhausted and really wanted to retire. They asked me to communicate their concern to Mr. Sui at intermission. Remembering my embarrassment with the snoring lady at the Leningrad Folk Dances back in 1976, I thought going back to the hotel was not a bad idea. Mr. Sui arranged transportation back to the hotel. I hope we did not appear to be bad guests in the eyes of our hosts.

The July Fourth holiday started early with heavy rain as we loaded our luggage on the bus at 7:00 a.m. We visited a boarding school for special needs students where a chorus of blind students sang *Home on the Range* in reasonably acceptable English as a welcoming gesture. Another blind student played a very touching accordion solo which reminded Patricia and me of her playing the instrument in her youth. Although the students could not really see our responses to their efforts, we tried to show our appreciation through audible applause.

Yangzhou

Shortly after lunch, the rain had relented and we were ready to enjoy sightseeing as we left Nanjing on a four lane highway for what proved to be a long bus ride to Yangzhou. The highway soon reduced to two lanes, then to a wide single lane, and then to a muddy two-track path. Progress was slow because traffic was heavy, passing almost impossible, and waits for on-coming traffic to clear the road were long and often. Patricia and I were intrigued by local gooseherds tending grazing flocks on the shoulders of the road. Each gooseherd had a long slim pole which he gently used to guide the lead goose in the direction he wished for it to go. The rest of the flock simply followed their leader to a new patch of grass. In retrospect, the geese seemed easier to lead than some of my group at the time.

Not being farmers at heart, some in my group were not interested in country scenes and became very impatient. They decided that they didn't want to go to Yangzhou after all. Suddenly, I had a rebellion on my hands. They informally agreed on a spokesperson to go over my head to Mr. Sui and demand that we turn around. Poor Mr. Sui was bewildered. That people would openly question the authority of their leaders was inconceivable to him. I pointed out that we were to spend three days in Yangzhou where schools had been preparing for our visit since April. Lodging and meal accommodations were authorized there. We were not in America. If we turned around, we had no guarantee of accommodations or reservations for the next three nights back in Nanjing. We spent a silent trip the rest of the way. We finally arrived in Yangzhou late for a formal tea with the Provincial Labor Minister, Education Minister, and local city officials. We were assigned rooms in a government guest house.

We were also late for the visit to the jade carving factory scheduled for that afternoon, but the factory officials graciously guided us through the very interesting operations. They were carving everything from beads for jewelry to sculptured animals to jade relief decorations on wall hangings and folding room dividers with wooden black-lacquer frames. The biggest and best piece was being prepared as a gift to President Reagan, to be presented to him by diplomats on a state visit to Washington later in the year. The production plant employed over one thousand workers, providing day care on site for their children.

The formal dinner that evening included the six officials we had met at tea. Through the course of the meal, each one felt the need to present a toast, and of course, one of us had to respond. My group had sweetened up when they again realized they were important, and made appropriate remarks assuring our hosts that they were pleased to be there.

After the meal, we were invited outside for a fireworks celebration in honor of our Independence Day. We stood on the front steps of the building while some young fellows lighted firecrackers in the front yard. Then to my surprise, a macho competition developed based on who dared hold the largest firecracker in his hands as it exploded. They started with really small ones and then moved closer to our group as the contest progressed. Anticipating where this contest was going, I quietly stepped to the rear of our group. The last Chinese to hold an exploding firecracker was obviously in pain as he hurried out of sight. His fellow showman lit a big one and handed it quickly to Jim Coody, who happened to be in the front line of my group. Poor Jim didn't drop it fast enough to avoid getting some minor, but painful, burns on his hand. I didn't think this was any way to treat guests. Perhaps we had witnessed a cultural tradition since the Chinese were the first to produce firecrackers.

The Chinese people in the Yangzhou area had little contact with foreigners. We were told that they would be curious about us, that they did not have the sense of private personal space that we did, and that they meant no harm when they approached us and felt our clothes or touched the skin of our hands and arms. While one professional exchange was taking place, I sent Patricia to a refreshment stand to get me a soft drink. Young fellows who had been playing volley ball nearby left their game and crowded around her as she made her purchase. They even stuck their noses into her large purse as she took out her money.

She did not like their curiosity, but remembering the warning we had been given, tried hard not to react negatively.

The morning of our first presentations in Yangzhou, my homemade transformer was very valuable. We were scheduled for simultaneous sessions in three different rooms. I got an overhead projector running for one group, then a slide projector for the second one. When I connected the last slide projector, I blew the power for the whole building. OH, OH! I disconnected the third projector while Mr. Sui found someone to replace the fuse or trip a circuit breaker to restore power. My little portable voltmeter told me that the voltage was too high for normal operation of my equipment, causing them to draw too much current (somewhere between our 120-volt and 220-volt systems). I theorized that there might be current capacity enough in the building if I used my homemade transformer to step down the voltage to a minimum operating level. I connected the transformer to the building power, adjusted the output voltage to 100 volts, RMS, connected one projector to the transformer directly, and connected the others with long extension cords I had with me. I crossed my fingers and turned on the projectors one at a time. They worked!

All the time I was setting up to run the projectors, the representative from the China Association of Science and Technology was watching my every move. After the presentations, he asked me through an interpreter how my power box worked. I determined that he had some training in electricity, so I showed him a schematic of the project to help explain its operation. He indicated that the Association needed such a device and asked me if I would sell it. I told him that I would be happy to give it to them at the end of our tour when we would no longer need it, if he could get authorization to clear my exit declaration form so that I could leave the country without it. He said he could get the authorization I needed. He did, and I was happy to leave that much weight behind me in China.

We received our best welcome at one of the schools in Yangzhou. This school featured a modern sewing laboratory and an Apple computer laboratory teaching the BASIC computer language. Different student groups, dressed in very colorful local costumes, presented a floor show of light ballet, singing, and folk dances. It was evident they had practiced long and hard. On the chalk board in big, artistic lettering were the words, "Warmly Welcome American Teachers!" I wondered how this reception made my rebellious crew feel. However, none of them ever apologized to me, or to my knowledge, to Mr. Sui.

Observations during the excursion to Yangzhou provided more examples of industrious human labor among the common people. The brick from a barge on the bank of the Yellow River was being unloaded by a human conveyer line, each worker handing a brick to the next person. Bare-footed construction workers climbed and worked on scaffolding erected from big, round bamboo poles placed horizontally about a foot apart where we would have used flat planks. Their bare feet gave them a better grip on the slippery poles. A superhighway was being built, not by bulldozers, road graders, and dump trucks, but by an army of workers with picks, shovels, and shoulder yokes to balance and remove paired buckets of excavated dirt. In contrast to what I had observed in Communist Russia years before, they appeared cheerfully energetic. Economic participation and progress was apparently providing personal rewards for their labor.

Following the last evening Exchange Dinner in Yangzhou, I became violently ill with food poisoning and had to miss the next day's activities. We learned that a few of the Chinese had also become sick, and that Mr. Sui's assistant had to be taken to the hospital. The concerned Chinese sent in a doctor with a little black bag to treat me. By then, I felt I had already emptied everything within me one way or the other, so I assured him I would be all right without further treatment. They sent in a "special breakfast for sick folk" which looked like a combination of green chicken noodle and egg drop soup. Now, I really was not hungry! I had Patricia secretly dispose of the soup. I did not want to hurt their feelings. I also skipped the morning's activities before boarding the bus back to Nanjing in the afternoon.

Goodbye to China

We flew out after lunch the next day, arriving in Guangzhou in time enough to settle into the Baiyun Hotel before going to our final dinner with top officials of the Chinese Association of Science and Technology. In the lobby, we met a party of forty Americans just starting on a People to People Ambassador's tour. I felt good to be a veteran answering the questions of the nervous neophytes.

The final dinner was full of diplomacy and good will. There were many toasts expressing their happiness that we had come to visit China, and our responses that we had learned much. They apologized profusely that I had become ill, and I assured them that I understood that such events happened once in a while in spite of the best intentions. The dinner's main course was also a unique way to serve fowl. They had dressed a duck as we would and then stretched out the body on a meat saw table to slice it crossways across flesh, bones, and cartilage, as we would slice a loaf of bread, from its head to its feet. The slices were re-assembled, and the duck, looking quite intact, was seasoned and baked. Each diner was served a complete slice of the duck. Patricia and I were served slices from the middle. The duck tasted very good.

By 11:00 the following morning, we were on the train enjoying the view of flat, lush green rice fields enclosed by low tree-capped hills with outcroppings of rock in the country between Guangzhou and Hong Kong. We had been through customs, currency exchange, passport, and visa checks without problems. I had a feeling of satisfaction that the Exchange had been successful in achieving our goals.

After my illness, I, especially, was ready for the next few days of rest and relaxation scheduled in Hong Kong. Although the China-US Scientific Exchanges had booked accommodations and some group activities, once we arrived there, I would no longer be the responsible leader. A weight had been taken from my shoulders.

Hong Kong

The Lee Garden Hotel, where we stayed in Hong Kong, was a beautiful, multi-story building with a polished stone exterior and very modern furnishings in the rooms. A large gift basket of fresh fruit, pears, peaches, bananas, apples, strawberries, oranges and even a pineapple greeted Patricia and me as we entered. We rested, unpacked,

Revealing the Unseen Hand

did laundry, and enjoyed a Big Mac hamburger with fries at a nearby McDonald's fast food restaurant!

In the morning we took a scheduled bus tour of the downtown area. We had never seen so many neon signs. People were living over the street level businesses in skyscraper-like apartment buildings. At many levels, laundry hung on pulley-operated lines stretched across the streets. The lines were apparently community property controlled by either end. The last stop on the tour was Stanleyville on the shore of the South China Sea. It was a picturesque tourist village with shopkeepers of all types selling anything one could imagine.

We took a tour of the intercity canals and waterways on an inflatable, motor-powered sampan. This was a grand adventure. There appeared to be hundreds of other sampans, all loaded with tourists attempting to share the same water surface. They bounced off from us, and we bounced off from them. At waterway intersections, there were no observable traffic rules as we had noticed on Holland's canals. Our pilot just kept aiming at the desired exit across the junction, shoving and being shoved in random directions until we popped out and went on our way. Everyone on our craft, and those whose faces we could see on the other sampans, seemed to be enjoying the experience. Patricia said, "This is bumper cars on water!" The sampan took us on a tour into the living areas of the boat people. These people lived on barges along the canal banks, just as those we had seen in the Netherlands.

Our party was scheduled for lunch at the top of Victoria Peak, the only mountain on the island of Hong Kong. A cable-pulled tram took us up the steep, three-mile track to the top where we enjoyed a grand view over the blue waters of the South China Sea. Other small green islands could be seen in the distance. Lunch was unremarkable, but the bus ride back down was white knuckles all the way. The bus took us to a jewelry factory where we enjoyed watching the artisans cutting, polishing, and mounting diamonds for a wide variety of pieces. Their work could be purchased at wholesale prices from a showroom, but Patricia and I didn't buy anything.

Lee R. Clendenning, PhD

Going home via Hawaii

We flew to Tokyo on the morning of July 7, 1985, and then on to Hawaii. A grass-skirted girl placed a lei around each of our necks as we left our plane. We walked along the beachfront, drove around Diamond Head, stopped at a pineapple farm, and visited the Arizona Memorial during our three day stay there before flying on to Atlanta via San Francisco and Minneapolis. Chip met us at midnight, and took us to the motel. At the motel, we were surprised and pleased to see that he had ordered a beautiful bouquet of fresh flowers with a card bearing the message: "Happy Birthday Mom, Welcome Home, Mom and Dad." He has always been a thoughtful son. We drove back to Rome the next afternoon, tired but pleased to have completed the circle.

Chapter 25

Completing a Career

In the years after my China trip and my return to Berry, there were a number of evolutionary changes in American society and professional organizations which forced changes in the curriculum, operating procedures, and to some extent even the traditional mission of Berry College. I continued to teach my classes and develop the curricula in my domain with limited resources. I also continued to serve the professional organizations. But eventually, the institution closed the industrial based programs and moved me into the Department of Mathematical and Computer Sciences. In my early sixties, I retrained myself to teach current computer technology through graduate classes at Southern Polytechnic and State University in Marietta, Georgia. In 2004, the younger faculty in the Department elected me to the chairmanship for two terms before I retired in the spring of 2010.

Retirement Celebrated

The School of Mathematical and Natural Sciences provided a royal celebration of my retirement. The School Executive Secretary, Mrs. Nina Wheeler, with help from Patricia, spent a lot of time (secretly from me) gathering pictures, diploma copies, public relations articles, administrative documents, certificates from workshops, and letters of appreciation from former students. Nina organized the memorabilia into chronological order and mounted it in a big scrapbook describing my thirty-seven year career at Berry. It was a grand work of love, presented to me at the official afternoon retirement reception. All of the Berry community, former students listed in the Alumni directory, my pastor and church friends were invited. Chip, his wife, Donna, my grandchildren, Victoria and Sterling, and Richard were there. My brother, Andy and his family also came to share in my moment. Dr. Bruce Conn, Dean of the School, acted as Master of Ceremonies. Many faculty colleagues and former students had nice things to say. The sweetest tribute came from Victoria who said that she was proud of her Grandfather and loved him very much. Nina knew that I was subject to vertigo, so I was presented with a regular oak retirement chair with plaque, rather than a rocker. Finger foods were served. I was later presented the traditional rocking chair by Berry College at the Annual Faculty-Staff Appreciation Banquet.

CHAPTER 26

FINDING A CHURCH HOME IN GEORGIA

Looking back over our years in Georgia, parallel to my professional success, Patricia and I experienced difficulty finding a place of long term acceptance, fellowship, and service in a home church. Three different churches we visited a number of times used a semi-friendly tactic to convey their apparent lack of comfort with us. After each Sunday morning service, different individuals would stop us in the parking lot and ask where we lived. When told, they would stroke their chin and say, kind of doubtfully, "I guess we do serve that area." Local folks did not understand that a college professor would still have a personal identity rooted in the working class. As the years went by, we acclimated better to the Southern culture. During the same period, with the influx of more people from the outside, the Southern culture became much less class-oriented and more tolerant of each other and intruders. Today's Georgia is vastly different than it was in the 1970s.

We did serve for extended periods in four different churches; both of us taught classes, Patricia sometimes played piano, and we sang in the choirs. I increased my ministry to hospitalized folk. As we floundered for the last time, visiting new churches and praying for guidance, we remembered a faithful choir director of our early days in Rome. We knew that Reverend Fred Barr was then Director of Music at Pleasant Valley South Baptist Church. We visited there and were well-received. That week we stopped for lunch at a cafeteria that we had visited only once in 25 years. Marjorie Barr, Fred's wife, just happened to be there and invited us to join her. She described the ministry of the church in such glowing terms that we were further intrigued. I learned later that in addition to being Church Pianist, she was the Pastor's Secretary. As we continued to visit, we were pleasantly surprised to find that many of our friends from a couple of churches where we had worked previously were now active there. We felt the fellowship of inclusion for the first time since we had arrived in Georgia! The Pastor, Dr. Phillip May, didn't seem intimidated to have me in the audience. The congregation was a mixture of working class and professional people. Dr. May preached the word with obviously careful and thoughtful preparation. We soon joined the fellowship and have been working there since 1999.

Our work in the church has been personally very fulfilling. Patricia and I co-teach a third-grade Sunday school class. We both sing in the Choir, and I have served two terms on the Active Deacon Board. I continue hospital calling, but at a greatly reduced frequency since my heart problems. We both participate in the fellowship activities of the "Prime Timers." With help from others, I developed and provided craft projects for Vacation Bible School for a number of years. My age and health, as well as the size and pressure of the task, have forced me to relinquish this responsibility.

Chapter 27
Health and Family

Although the auto-accident as a teenager affected the whole direction of my life, requiring an academic career, I went through years when the back injury was not on the forefront of my mind. However, during the late 1980s, I began to carry heavier loads, forgot to monitor my long-term sitting positions, and gained some weight, all of which may have contributed to a resurgence of serious back pain and loss of some control in my legs. Because my students needed me, we rented a wheelchair, and I started teaching from it. My students were sympathetic and helped by pushing me around. I started using transparencies with an overhead projector instead of the chalkboard.

I consulted an orthopedic surgeon, who ordered a CT scan of my spine. He reported that scar tissue was pressuring tangled nerves in one of the lumbar disks. There was a combination of older damage and more recent disk problems. He recommended swimming and extended physical therapy, and further, I was to stand as much as possible and to sit only when absolutely necessary. If I did sit, I was to use a chair with armrests so that I could bear some of my weight with my forearms and elbows. Because surgery would entail a great risk of permanent paralysis, he would not attempt it unless my legs became completely paralyzed.

We returned the wheelchair and moved a pulpit-style speaker's stand into my office to work at much of the time instead of my desk. I joined the YMCA and started swimming there for an hour each morning at 6:00. At church, I stood in the back. Slowly, I recovered capabilities.

I was again thankful for the advice I had been given as a teenager to prepare to support myself with my brain and not my brawn. I was also again thankful for God's Unseen Hand in making my academic career possible. Today, if I sit too long in one position, I start to lose control of my legs. I let Patricia drive on all out of town trips, and we stop often for a physical stretch.

Chip and Richard's careers

As he was finishing his Master's Degree studies at Georgia Tech, Chip decided that he really wanted to teach mathematics. With our encouragement, he moved home and enrolled in professional teacher education courses at Berry College to achieve certification. He has been teaching mathematics for Gainesville College, Gainesville, Georgia since 1990. Chip married the former Donna Beam, a Berry alumnus and high school English teacher, on July 27, 1991. They are the parents of our grandchildren, Victoria Leigh and Sterling Leigh. We are proud of all of them!

After graduation with a Master's Degree from Georgia Tech, Richard worked in engineering positions before spending 17 years teaching electronics and computer technology for Clayton State College. When the 1996 Olympics were being planned, he obtained a year's leave of absence from Clayton State to train audio-visual technicians to operate electronic equipment needed to provide commentary systems at the various competitive venues. That program ended before Christmas in 1995. Early in the winter of 1996, he suddenly had time on his hands. He somehow arranged a temporary English teaching assignment at the Moscow State Pedagogical University in Russia. This southern boy went there in the middle of the winter and, by his reports, nearly froze to death. He returned home in June of 1996. After the Olympics, Richard returned to teaching for Clayton State.

Richard married the former Jodi (Sasha) Gorham of Detroit, Michigan on July 30, 2000. I understand they met due to their mutual interest in Russia while Sasha was a student at Clayton State. They both embraced the Orthodox Church, and in that church, they are known as Paul and Aleksandra Clendenning, following the New Testament convention of changing a first name when one joins the Church.

Richard continues to study more topics than I can recall. In 2007, he returned to private employment, this time in the area of computer network security.

Given more Life after a botched heart operation!

In the middle of the night in the spring of 2007, I awoke to symptoms of heart trouble. In due time, after many tests, I was scheduled for a quadruple bypass operation. I went into surgery on a Friday morning and was moved to recovery in the evening. The surgeon told Patricia that I still "had a small bleeder;" but he was confident it would correct itself in time. I regained consciousness enough to know I was still alive, and that Patricia and Chip were both with me. Richard had been trapped in interstate traffic. Then, either I went back to sleep or lost consciousness. Told that there was nothing more they could do and that I probably would not be conscious again until morning, Patricia and Chip went home to rest.

I understand it was past 10:00 p.m. when the surgeon had an operator interrupt a phone conversation between Chip and his wife, Donna, to say that I was still bleeding and that he would need to re-open my chest to repair the leak. They were to return to the hospital immediately. Patricia took the time to call Mark Winstead, our Minister of Music, to request that my condition be placed on the Church Prayer Chain. When she arrived at the hospital, Mark was there; a number of others including our Pastor, Dr. Phillip May, soon arrived. While the surgeon worked to correct whatever mistake he had made, these good folks held prayer for me in the waiting room. An attending nurse later told us that my blood pressure had dropped to 50/30: "We thought we had lost him!" Apparently, God had more need of me here than in Heaven. I am humbled to realize I am living on additional time granted as an answer to prayer. I am trying to make good use of that time!

Lee R. Clendenning, PhD

50'Th Wedding Celebration

Patricia and I had been married for 50 years on June 6, 2009. We celebrated by having a family portrait taken of us, our sons, their wives, and the grandchildren which hangs on our living room wall in a walnut frame which I had made. We reserved a room for a banquet in the Landmark Restaurant in Rome, Georgia. Donna, with help from Chip and Victoria, decorated the tables with beautiful flower arrangements and the walls with a "Happy 50'th Anniversary, Lee and Patricia" banner and a photo display of highlights in our family history. These items were subsequently moved to the walls of our home.

In addition to our immediate family, in attendance were my brother Andy Clendenning, his wife Carol, one of their sons, Mike Clendenning, and one of their daughters, Janice Hartford. Patricia's brother Douglas Terrill, his wife Linda, and one of their daughters, Cindy, attended. Victoria Clendenning had everyone sign the Guest Book for us. After the meal, we all retired to our home for further fellowship and reminiscing. It was a wonderful day of celebration; my cup was running over with the appreciation of blessings.

Back, Left to right: Lee, Jr., Donna, Lee, Sasha, Richard
Front: Sterling, Patricia, Victoria

Chapter 28

The Unseen Hand Has Been Revealed!

My reflections on some of the wondrous events of my life, which I have documented in this narrative, and a lifetime of observations of others, have led me to some conclusions. Much, but not all, of the functions of the Unseen Hand are carried out by good, well-meaning people, walking in the light they have been given, doing their jobs with commendable concern for the welfare of others. They are the salt of the earth (Matthew 5:13) who love their neighbor as themselves (Matthew 22:39) even if they do not personally know those neighbors. The person who called me out of the shop to take my scholarship test undoubtedly knew me, but the Director of Admissions, who argued for three hours that I should be given a chance, must have been such a person. Mr. Loper was such a person. People who contribute to the benevolence program of their churches are part of the Unseen Hand preparing to meet the future critical need of someone at a critical point in that person's life. Anonymous giving was specifically approved by Jesus when he said, ". . . let not your right hand know what your left hand doeth." (Matthew 6:3). There are people (and I am one) who say to one of the church leaders, "I know that so and so's family has a critical need; please give them this contribution, but don't tell them where it came from." When I learned that a Berry student was living in the back seat of his car because he could not afford to live in the dorm, I called the Director of Physical Plant and asked him, "On Berry's 30,000 acres, don't you have an empty cottage or cabin somewhere that needs more night-time security?" Of course, he asked why I was so personally interested in campus security. I then explained the student's situation, and he found such a place for the student to live. The last I heard from that student, he was a county vocational education supervisor. Being part of God's Unseen Hand for someone else is personally fulfilling!

There are exceptions to my general observation that God's purpose is achieved through well-meaning people. Joseph's brothers' actions placed him in Egypt in position to save his family from famine. My interactions with my jealous freshmen peer, the promise of the Spirit that the student would call me one day, and the actual confirming call, strengthened my faith. The wonder of the Unseen Hand is that such people and events can be used to fulfill God's plan in spite of their own personal motivations.

One often hears or reads some version of St. Teresa of Avila's motivational teaching:

> Christ has no body now on earth but yours,
> no hands but yours,
> no feet but yours,
> yours are the eyes through which Christ's compassion
> is to look out to the earth,
> yours are the feet by which He is to go about doing good
> and yours are the hands by which He is to bless us now.
> (http://www.rc.net/southwark/ashfordstteresa/St%20Teresa%20of%20Avila.htm)

St. Teresa is correct with respect to Christ's physical body; however, her teaching should not be interpreted as a limitation of God's power on earth. God's Spirit was able to tell me where to purchase a mobile home without any other human intermediary. The Spirit gave me an epiphany of His life-long actions on my behalf at the Great Wall. The Power that sharpened David's aim at Goliath, closed the mouths of lions for Daniel, brought the three Hebrew children out of the furnace, healed the sick, and raised Lazarus from the dead is fully active today and not limited by the actions (or inactions) of me or anybody else. I have experienced that Power!

While passing through the State of Tennessee on our way to New York, Patricia was driving east on a four-lane highway which had an additional center turning lane. Looking ahead, we both saw a vehicle coming from the west at a very high speed. As the distance between us closed, at the last instant, when it was too late for Patricia to take any meaningful defensive action, the driver made what appeared to be a suicidal, head-on attack. The vehicle crossed the traffic lanes. Without time to pray, somehow I was prepared to die. Just before what should have been the impact, defying all of Newton's laws of physics about bodies in motion, the attacking vehicle was suddenly shoved (not steered) **_sideways to our left_**!, the direction he had been coming from. We came to an emergency stop as the vehicle disappeared behind us. Don't tell me God has only my hands to work with! This event meets C. S. Lewis's definition of a miracle:

"I use the word *miracle* to mean an interference with Nature by supernatural power." (*Miracles*, C. S. Lewis, ISBN 978-0-06-065301-9, 1947, p. 5.)

The narrative of my life is not over; I know in my heart that life means more than Shakespeare's character described it:

. . . a tale
told by an idiot,
full of sound and fury,
signifying nothing. (Macbeth, Act 5, Scene 5)

Only God knows what lies ahead in the time that I have been given. My deepest desires are that the knowledge of the miracles worked by the Unseen Hand will not die with me and that readers will walk in the light they have been given, finding fulfillment as God works out His purpose in their lives. Looking back on my life, I can see that the prophesy of Isaiah—that a path for a wayfaring person would be made so plain that a fool would not err therein—was fulfilled! (Isaiah 35:8) I agree with Solomon: ". . . Fear God, and keep His commandments: for this is the whole duty of man." (Ecclesiastes 12:13b)

CPSIA information can be obtained at www.ICGtesting.com
Printed in the USA
LVOW07s1107270515

440071LV00001B/14/P